16.

INTO
HARMONY
WITH THE
PLANET

INTO
HARMONY
WITH THE
PLANET

*The delicate balance between industry
and the environment*

Michael Allaby

Foreword by David Puttnam

The preparation of this book has been supported by the ICI Group
Environmental Laboratory at Brixham in Devon to mark the opening
of a major new extension to the Laboratory.

First published 1990

Text copyright © Michael Allaby

Copyright © Bloomsbury Publishing Limited

Bloomsbury Publishing Limited, 2 Soho Square, London W1V 5DE

A CIP record for this title is available from the British Library.

ISBN 07475 06213

Edited, designed, and produced by Curtis Garratt Limited, The Old
Vicarage, Horton-cum-Studley, Oxford OX9 1BT.

Picture research by Jennifer Garratt

Index by Neil Curtis Publishing Services

Printed in Spain by Artes Gráficas Toledo, S.A.
D.L.TO:1041-1990

CONTENTS

Acknowledgements

Ecological Consultant:
Ken Smith M Phil., LRSC, M I Inf. Sc.

The production of this book has been helped by numerous
individuals from many companies. To all we give our sincere
thanks. In particular:
C. Craig; J. R. Finney; R. W. Hill; J. R. Lawrence; G. B. Lewis; J.
F. D. Mills; R. C. Pocock; D. Riley; R. T. Robson; R. Walters; M.
Wiseman from ICI. Also ICI's companies world wide especially
ICI Australia Operations Pty Ltd, ICI Argentina, ICI Japan, ICI
Wilhelmshaven, West Germany (Gerhard Czieslik).

In addition we would like to thank:
Peter Evans; British Petroleum; British Gas; British Telecom;
English China Clays; Conoco Inc, Houston Texas (Terry L.
Thoem); C.S.M.E., Salin de Giraud, France (M. Claude Febure);
Dow Chemical, Texas (John Harrison); Florida Power and Light
Co, Florida (D. Greg Braun and J. Ross Wilcox); Florida Panther
National Wildlife Refuge (Todd Logan); Nairobi, Kenya (Anne
and Gordon Davies); State of Florida Department of Transporta-
tion (Gary L. Evink); Kennedy Space Center, NASA, Florida; and
The Magadi Soda Company, Kenya.

Preface

❛ The end of the nineteen eighties will, I'm sure, always be re-
membered for the way in which environmental issues were precipitated to
the forefront of public attention. A little like Henry Boot's memorable ex-
periences in Evelyn Waugh's *Scoop*. the innocent writers of 'Nature Notes'
on the domestic pages of daily newspapers suddenly found themselves
thrust on to the front page!

But as this book reminds us, environmentalism has been around
for *much* longer than that. For decades, committed individuals and organizations have laboured to convince hostile or simply apathetic interests that
the environment mattered. The harsh truth is that they have failed, and
that failure derives as much from ill-conceived compromises as from the
outright rejection of environmental arguments.

A number of such compromises are described in this book, but it
also shows how success can emerge when environmental concerns are
genuinely understood, and serious attempts are made to integrate them
from the outset.

If the eighties were the decade of environmental awareness, the
nineties will be the decade in which society will have to decide once and
for all on its priorities, if not even its imperatives. It is a sad irony that if we
fail to define completely new solutions, attitudes and measurements of
progress, at this time of relative prosperity, unprecedented public enthusi-
asm for the environment and a corporate willingness to develop new ways
of working, we may never again capture the opportunity to do so.

This book is an important contribution to the process that will enable us to distinguish between the false compromises and the genuinely
new solutions which *must* emerge if we are to face the future with anything approaching confidence. ❜

INTRODUCTION
THE CHANGING LANDSCAPE

Once upon a time, glaciers and ice sheets extended over most of the land in latitudes higher than about 50 degrees north. The sea was frozen and, further south, sea levels were low enough for land animals to walk between what are now France, Britain and Ireland, and between Alaska and Siberia. The advancing ice had destroyed all plant life and scoured away the very soil in which the plants once grew. As the climate grew warmer, the ice retreated to reveal a bare, empty landscape. Beyond the edge of the ice lay a belt of tundra, of frozen soil where its surface thawed in summer to produce shallow lakes and marshes, supporting a sparse vegetation of herbs and small, stunted bushes. Beyond the tundra lay vast coniferous forests and, beyond them, deciduous broadleaved forest. Following the retreat of the ice, these vegetational belts migrated northwards as the wind and birds deposited seeds in places that were now warm and moist enough for them to germinate. Until the rising sea

A glacier on the Jungfrau mountain, in Switzerland. It is only about 10 000 years since glaciers retreated from many of the valleys of northern Europe, Asia, and North America.

level produced what we now see as islands, the plants were followed by the animals associated with them.

It all happened before the dawn of our written history and it seems a very long time ago. Yet it was not so long ago, in fact no more than about 10 000 years since the ice retreated, and that is a very short time for a planet with a history that extends over billions of years. Nor was it the first time the ice had advanced and then retreated, and it may not be the last!

We like to think of the familiar landscapes around us as eternal, but it is an illusion. They change naturally, over periods that are long only when measured against the brief span of a human life. The

As a species, humans are a phenomenal success.

arrival of humans brings further changes, and more rapidly. One thousand years ago, most of northern Europe, including Britain, was forested, but even then the forests were being cleared. New landscapes were emerging, produced by farmers who needed land to grow crops and graze livestock, and wood was the principal fuel used not only to warm homes and to cook food but also to smelt ores and to forge metals.

As a species, humans are a phenomenal success. Our numbers have increased, and

continue to increase, due very largely to our skill in modifying our surroundings to make them more hospitable. The rainforests of Colombia provide tribal people with everything they need, but at a sustainable population density of about one person to every 1000 hectares (2500 acres). In the United Kingdom, 1000 hectares supplies the needs of more than 2000 people.

In the regions where humans have settled and where civilizations have developed, little of the original, 'natural' countryside remains. It has been transformed into plantation forest, farmland, and towns and cities. The grasslands of North and South America and of Africa may well have resulted from the fires lit by humans to drive game, and the North American prairies are now farms, growing cereals — grasses with ancestors that came from the Near East. The countryside we see is the product of human endeavour — of human industry.

Yet the seas and oceans cover more than two-thirds of the surface of the Earth, confining us to the remaining third, and only part of that is readily available to us. Large areas remain

Above: Beyond the edge of the ice sheets lay tundra landscapes, like this one in the Richardson Mountains, Yukon. Below: A farming landscape in Devon, made by humans since the ice age ended.

Rainforest, the richest of all habitats. This is in Colombia.

Damage has certainly been inflicted although now, many years after the event, we do not always find the result unattractive. The clearance of forests and exploitive farming methods have created bleak upland moors in high latitudes, treasured now as open spaces and often protected from further development. In the Mediterranean region, the same causes led to widespread soil erosion and produced landscapes that now attract tourists by the million. Land abandoned and left derelict years ago by the closure of mines, quarries, and factories has been colonized by wildlife in some places, to make landscapes that many people regard as entirely natural. In other places, the historical interest of old sites has led to their restoration for the entertainment of us all.

Archaeologists will find it much more difficult, and perhaps impossible, to

> *... we no longer consider ourselves entitled to ignore the effects on the environment ...*

determine the precise location of the manufacturing sites we use today. Attitudes have changed and we no longer consider ourselves entitled to ignore the effects on the environment as we extract the materials we need and process them into the things we use. We have changed our attitude because we have learned more about the consequences of our activities. We know, as our forefathers did not always know, that the discharge of certain substances into the air or water is harmful, eventually to ourselves. We have come to appreciate our need for attractive, clean surroundings in which to work and relax, and the role played by wild plants and animals in providing those surroundings. A clean, safe environment has a value, even if we cannot yet express

unsettled, and little affected by human activities, because they resist our attempts to wrest a living from them. The tundra regions and, beyond them, the polar regions are too cold for us to grow our food crops, and the deserts too dry. The mountains are often too steep to be cultivated and the soil is too thin. The soils of the tropical forests are infertile, and the climate is so warm and wet that such poor crops as can be grown are quickly choked by opportunist weeds or devoured by insects. Our influence on our surroundings is great, but it is tightly concentrated. This means that such environmental harm as we inflict is mainly confined to the regions we have settled, but in those regions it may be severe.

that value in precise economic terms. As our appreciation of the natural environment has grown, so has our skill in limiting the injuries we inflict on it. A modern factory, operated by an enlightened management, is planned in such a way as to minimize its adverse environmental effect, and the planning extends to the time when the factory reaches the end of its useful life, is closed and then demolished, and the ground on which it stood is restored for some other use. Where such planning is successful — and it is improving all the time — within a few years of its closure, there need be no visible evidence that the factory ever existed. That is why future archaeologists may need to devise

The Serengeti National Park, in Tanzania, where the vast expanses of the savanna grasslands support large herds of grazing animals, including the wildebeest seen here; their migrations follow the seasonal rains that regenerate the pasture.

new and much more subtle techniques than they possess today if they are to find the traces they seek.

In this book, I trace some of the ways in which our industrial activities have altered the environment. It is not my purpose to suggest that all is perfect, that there is no ugly or badly sited factory, or that pollution of the environment by factory discharges has ceased. Clearly that is not the case, but there is another side to the story, one of which we hear less and one that I believe should be told.

Human industry exists for the benefit of humans so, when we consider its effects on the environment, we should not ignore the human environment in which, by and large, we live longer, are healthier, better fed, clothed, housed, informed, and generally more comfortable than we would be without this environmental

*... we live longer,
are healthier, better fed,
clothed, housed, informed,
and generally more
comfortable ...*

intervention. The book is arranged, therefore, in chapters, each of which reflects a particular human need, the way it has been and is satisfied, and the past and present consequences for the natural environment, and especially for wildlife, of satisfying it. I begin with water, the most fundamental of our requirements, and proceed to food, clothing, timber, stone, fuel, power, minerals and materials, chemicals, and transport and communication. Then I discuss waste disposal. Many of the examples I describe illustrate the skill with which land can now be restored,

not necessarily to its former state but for any of a range of uses chosen during the initial planning stage by the communities that will use it when its industrial use ends. Where factories are built on land that has previously been used for industrial purposes and has been left derelict, this allows wasteland to pass through an industrial regeneration and eventually to be returned much improved from its former condition.

The book ends with two chapters describing more specifically the ways in which industrial activities have been directly beneficial to wildlife. The first deals with wildlife on industrial sites, the species that arrive of their own accord and are then encouraged and protected. It is no longer unusual to find a bird sanctuary or nature reserve on, or adjacent to, an industrial site or to find industrial land

Olive groves at Phaestos, Greece, thriving in a landscape where the rugged beauty is due to the severe soil erosion that followed the clearance of the forests which once grew here.

being managed jointly by company executives and conservationists.

The second deals with the rare species that sometimes arrive, or are discovered, on industrial sites. There are several examples of these. American crocodiles nest in the cooling water of a Florida power station, for example; whooping cranes feed on land owned by an oil company; natterjack toads live on several British industrial sites, including one on land owned by British Nuclear Fuels; and, perhaps most extraordinary of all, one of the rarest birds in the world is to be found in Australia on land owned by one of the world's largest chemical companies. In each case, the company concerned has reacted by providing the best and most carefully protected habitat possible for the species of which, invariably, the company is extremely proud.

The book ends with a brief outline of 'sustainable development' and its implications. This concept was introduced some years ago but its details and practical applications have yet to be defined. The idea of 'sustainability' is widely accepted by industrialists in principle because it is not alien to them. They accept the wisdom of extracting as much value as they can from resources, which is a way of husbanding them; they are accustomed to long-term planning, and modern planning has to take account of the environmental consequences of any industrial operation.

What is surprising is not that industrial managers are learning to exercise environmental responsibility, but that anyone should find this remarkable. Originally, the word 'industry' was applied to individuals to describe the diligence and skill with which they work. Today, many of us associate the word with machines, ugly buildings, dirt, and environmental degradation. People barely enter the definition. This is unfortunate because it is misleading. Those machines are designed, built, managed, and operated by human beings — it is their skill and diligence that makes

them 'industrious' — and the machines are but tools, used to supply us with the goods that form the basis of our way of life. The people who work in 'industry' are no different from those who pursue other careers. They are as likely as anyone else to be keen on art or music, sport or foreign travel — or on the protection of the environment. The staff of industrial companies includes a similar proportion of naturalists to that found in other working environments and, these days, some of those naturalists have been trained professionally. Botanists, zoologists, and ecologists are employed to study the environmental effects of industrial processes and products. They are hardly likely to accept without protest the destruction of natural habitats.

Environmentalists and conservationists have expressed very fluently their concern at the present state of the global environment and their fears for its future. In doing so they have established an agenda, but one whose items they alone cannot resolve. Success, measured as a steady improvement in the standard of living of most of the people of the world accompanied by a parallel improvement in the condition of the natural environment, can be achieved only through the close collaboration of scientists from many disciplines, industrial managers, and the environmentalists and conservationists themselves. If that goal can be attained, all of us will benefit; if not, all of us will suffer.

It is often supposed that the difference in outlook between industrialists and environmentalists has grown so wide as to make communication between them almost impossible. If this book exposes the error in that supposition, it will have achieved its principal aim. The agenda is a common agenda, and in many practical ways, often at a local level, quietly and unostentatiously, the collaboration is already producing genuine environmental improvements.

The Greenhouse Effect

The Sun bathes the surface of the Earth in radiation whose wavelength ranges from that of heat (long-wave) to ultra-violet (short-wave). Warmed by the Sun, the surface radiates heat. As it passes through the atmosphere some of this long-wave radiation is intercepted by certain gas molecules — principally carbon dioxide but also methane, chlorofluorocarbon compounds (CFCs) and several others. These molecules re-radiate the heat, warming the air. This warming, first suggested by scientists more than a century ago, is now known as the 'greenhouse effect' and the gases associated with it as 'greenhouse gases'.

Some 4 billion years ago the Sun was cooler than it is today but the atmosphere consisted mainly of carbon dioxide and the greenhouse effect warmed the climate enough for living organisms to establish themselves. Since then the Sun has grown warmer but the greenhouse effect has been reduced. Carbon dioxide has been removed from the air and 'buried' as carbonate rocks, such as limestone, and as peat, coal, natural gas, and petroleum.

GREENHOUSE GASES

We are now burning these fuels and returning the carbon dioxide to the air — currently at a rate of about 19 billion tonnes a year, and this rate is increasing. Since 1955 the amount of carbon dioxide in the air has risen by 10 per cent.

Methane is much rarer than carbon dioxide, but molecule for molecule it is a much more effective greenhouse gas and its concentration in the atmosphere is rising twice as fast. Methane is produced by bacteria in the digestive systems of ruminant animals — mainly cattle, but also sheep and goats — and termites. The intensification of live-stock farming has led to an increase in numbers of cattle, and deforestation in the tropics and subtropics has increased the amount of rotting wood on which termites feed, so their numbers have also increased.

Scientists believe that, eventually, our injection of greenhouse gases into the air will produce a climatic warming. It is too soon to tell whether that warming has already commenced. Nor do we yet know what all of its effects may be, but they are likely to be seriously disruptive. Agricultural patterns may change as more northerly lands become suitable for farm crops but areas further south become drier. Sea levels are likely to rise, though no-one knows by how much, threatening low-lying coastal areas with flooding.

FOUR TREES PER PERSON

President Bush has suggested that Americans plant four trees for every person living in the United States — nearly

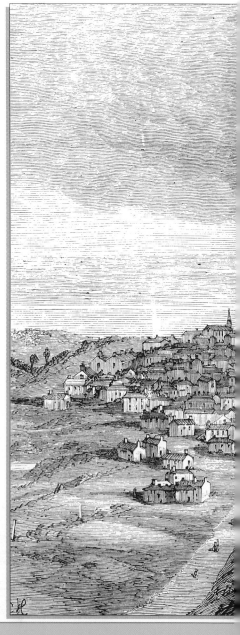

a billion trees. Such large-scale afforestation would absorb carbon dioxide as the trees grew but, when they died and decomposed or were felled and burnt, their carbon would be oxidized back into carbon dioxide. Unless felled or fallen timber was buried permanently, isolated from the atmosphere, afforestation could bring only a temporary respite.

If we are to reduce the rate at which we release greenhouse gases, we must alter our farming so there are fewer animals and find ways to prevent further deforestation in the tropics. Most of all, we must learn to burn less wood, peat, coal, natural gas, and oil. We can do this by reducing the amount of energy we use and by finding alternative energy sources.

The environment of industrial Europe and America has been improved. This is Dowlais, in Wales, as it was in 1875, when the factories belched smoke across the valley.

CHAPTER 1
WATER — AND THE LACK OF IT

Over much of the Sahara, as here in Morocco, the ground is hard and stony. The scattered plants are too tough and indigestible for farm animals other than goats.

The word 'wilderness' conjures for most of us an image of mountains, forests, or perhaps of high moorlands where rocks, expanses of heather, and botanically remarkable bogs are lashed by wind-driven rain. We live, most of us, crowded together in cities and we need to know such places still exist, those vast areas, empty of people, where we may find solitude and spiritual regeneration. It was

---

... *without water*
we will die ...

---

not always so. A few centuries ago our forefathers had little regard for these agriculturally unproductive landscapes.

Nor is it so today in those parts of the world where hardship and danger are facts of everyday life. The Arabic word for 'wilderness' is *sahrá*, which we transliterate into English as 'Sahara', the name of the largest desert in the world, a beautiful but dreadful region, where water is the most treasured resource. It is no coincidence that, among desert peoples, paradise is pictured as a well-watered garden.

We all know that without water we will die, but it is easy to underestimate the amount of water we must have simply to live. A few litres a day will supply us with as much as we need to drink, and a few more will allow us to wash and cook our food, but the food itself requires water. When you buy a kilogram of dry whole-meal flour, there is nothing on the label to tell you that it took about 1500 litres (330 gallons) of water simply to grow the wheat from which the flour was made — and wheat is by no means the most demanding of crops. It takes about 4000 litres (880 gallons) of water to produce 1 kilogram ($2^1/4$ pounds) of rice and about 10 000 (2200 gallons) to produce a kilogram of cotton fibre. Weigh a quantity of dried peas; then multiply the weight by 750 and you will have calculated the minimum weight of water that passed through the plants from which the peas were gathered. (1 litre of water weighs 1 kilogram; 1 gallon of water weighs 10 pounds.)

MAKING BEST USE OF WATER

From the earliest times, people have devised highly ingenious methods for conserving water where it was scarce, and for augmenting the ordinary supply where it was insufficient. In the Sahara itself, where two-thirds of the sparse population live in permanent settlements, many of the oases have been enlarged by human industry. In some places, gently sloping channels, called *foggaras*, run below the surface, collecting groundwater that flows to a central oasis. In other places, artesian wells are used to irrigate date palms and the other crops that grow in the shade they provide. In Egypt, only 1 per cent of all water enters the domestic supply. The remainder is used to irrigate farm crops.

Salination is the most serious danger arising from crop irrigation in warm climates. Plants and animals require fresh water and will die from dehydration should the water in their tissues become too saline. When land is irrigated by pouring or spraying water on to the surface some of the water will soak downwards, to the region of the plant roots, and some will evaporate from the surface. In a warm, dry climate, the rate of evaporation is high and, as the upper region of the soil dries, groundwater is drawn upwards by capillary attraction through the tiny spaces between soil particles. Groundwater is a weak solution of mineral salts that have dissolved out of the soil and underlying rocks. As water continues to evaporate from the surface, the salts are left behind and may accumulate. Heavy rain will wash them away but, where rainfall is light, the soil may

Even in dry regions there is often water below ground, if you dig deeply enough. Without irrigation using water from this borehole, at the Chitsuachirimutsaka Co-operative in Zimbabwe, farming would be impossible.

Automated irrigation, in Saudi Arabia, allows wheat to grow in the desert. As the booms rotate, water is sprayed from nozzles. It takes about 1500 litres (330 gallons) of water to grow enough wheat to produce 1 kilogram (2.2 pounds) of wholewheat flour.

eventually become sterile and, when the salts are washed from the soil they may pollute nearby rivers. Around Wentworth, South Australia, for example, every year farm irrigation brings up to 3000 tonnes of salts to the surface of each hectare (2.5 acres) of land and 2.5 tonnes of it flows into the Murray River every minute. In 1989, Prime Minister Bob Hawke announced a major programme to protect the Australian environment, delighting the National Farmers' Federation by placing particular emphasis on improved farming methods that would lead to the recovery of the saline lands and the waters of the Murray.

... *a major programme to protect the Australian environment,* ...

Perhaps it was the *foggaras* that inspired the inventors of a modern technique for preventing salination. The risk can be averted if the water is applied not to the surface, from which it may evaporate, but below ground, to the roots themselves. The water flows through small-diameter plastic pipes with outlets at intervals along them, the layout of the piping and frequency of outlets being determined by the crop that is to be irrigated. The system is called 'drip' or 'trickle' irrigation

because it uses so little water. Depending on the crop, each outlet may deliver about 4 litres (7 pints) an hour. This may sound a great deal but it is much less than overhead sprinkler systems use. Yields of some Israeli crops have doubled using half the water, and the method is widely used in Hawaii, as well as in India and other countries in the dry subtropics, mainly in orchards and vineyards and on sugar cane crops.

Drip irrigation would be impossible were there no plastics industry to produce cheap, durable piping. No other material serves the purpose so well or requires so little maintenance once it has been installed.

This is not the only contribution to agriculture that is made by industries not usually associated with farming. In many places, water is 'harvested' by collecting rainwater. The most efficient way to harvest water involves sealing the soil surface with asphalt or with industrially made silicone resins so that, instead of soaking in, all of the rainwater drains down a slope into a tank.

INCREASING THE SUPPLY

As human numbers increase in a particular area, demand for food and water increases in proportion. It is a situation with which we are familiar enough today, but we are not the first to experience it, nor the first to employ skilled engineers to devise means of increasing supplies.

Perhaps the most remarkable system is that which fed Mexico in the days of the Aztec empire. The city stood on an island in a shallow lake that was reduced to five small lakes during the dry season. Canals were dug to form a grid pattern and the mud from the excavation piled on the adjacent ground to make rectangular raised beds secured at first by fences and eventually by trees. Plant crops were grown very intensively on the resulting plots, called *chinampas*, and fish were cultivated in the water. The *chinampas* were fertilized with human wastes and received regular applications of mud and aquatic plants dredged from the canals to keep them open. Each plot was worked by one family and, although no records survive of the crop yields attained, people seem to have been well fed and, under Aztec rule, the growers were burdened with heavy taxes that were paid in produce. Salination did not occur because the water flowed through the canals from fresh-water springs and when, in the fifteenth century, these proved inadequate, causeways were built to bring water from further afield. A somewhat similar method, called 'uta culture', has been

In arid regions, irrigation water may be lost by soaking into the ground from the channels carrying it. This channel, in Quinghai Province, China, is being lined to conserve scarce water.

devised quite independently in Peru, using heavy duty polythene sheeting to line the canals and so prevent the loss of water.

It is the evaporation of salt or brackish water that causes salination but, by evaporating sea water and condensing the vapour, fresh water can be obtained from the sea. Solar energy can be used to heat the water but, more commonly, the desalination plant is combined with a power station. In the 2-hectare (5-acre) plant at Abu Dhabi, for example, the water is heated to produce steam which drives generating turbines; the outgoing hot water is used to preheat incoming sea water without mixing the two, and most of the condensed, cooled, fresh water is then fed to greenhouses and to a drip irrigation system outdoors. The Abu Dhabi plant produces about 265 000 litres (59 000 gallons) of fresh water a day and, in its first six months, the complex grew more than 200 tonnes of vegetables.

The possibilities of desalination have led

some people to imagine it might be used to irrigate large areas of what is now desert — to 'make the desert bloom'. Unfortunately, the water is much too expensive for this to be practicable. In years to come, perhaps, advances in the use of solar heat will allow the cost to fall but, for the time being, agriculture and horticulture can be fed from desalination plants only in such places as Abu Dhabi, where the oil industry provides at once a concentration of workers who must be fed and enough capital to construct the installation. Desalination has been considered for Britain, but desalinated sea water is estimated to cost up to fifteen times as much as fresh water from more conventional sources. This does not mean, however, that inexpensive ways may not be found to increase the efficiency of water use in arid regions.

WATER, WILDLIFE, AND INDUSTRY

The need to conserve water and to protect it from pollution can bring very direct benefits to wildlife. In The Gambia, for example, a small West African country that forms a narrow strip extending inland for about 480 kilometres (298 miles) to either side of the Gambia river, protection of the catchment (known in North America as the 'watershed') has allowed the

Abuko Forest to develop as a wildlife reserve.

The biological importance of water derives from its physical and chemical properties. The arrangement of the atoms

The association of water with industry is very ancient.

in water molecules is such that water readily forms temporary associations with a wide range of substances. This makes it an excellent solvent and, in the bodies of plants and animals, nutrients are transported in solution, and water is the medium in which many chemical reactions take place. When water freezes, melts, evaporates, or condenses, 'latent' heat is absorbed or released. It is the latent heat, supplied by the body to evaporate perspiration, that cools us. A dog, which has few sweat glands, pants to evaporate water from its tongue, mouth, and respiratory passages. These same properties make water a vital resource for industry.

The association of water with industry is very ancient. The flow of water can be used to turn a wheel. These days we call such a wheel a 'turbine', a word coined early in the last century and derived from the Latin *turbo* meaning 'a whirling object'. The first waterwheel is believed to have been invented in the first century BC Probably it was used to lift water for irrigation. The milling of grain came later, and windmills, a much more recent invention, evolved from the concept of the waterwheel. The first factories to be built in what was later called the Industrial Revolution were powered by water. When the waterwheels were replaced by

The red colobus monkey (Colobus badius), *seen here in the Abuko Forest, seldom moves far from water. Protecting the catchment to either side of the Gambia river has allowed the Forest to develop as a wildlife reserve, providing a habitat for many species.*

steam-powered engines, it was still water that was used and, of course, the development of steam power made it possible to build the locomotives that gave us the first high-speed transport network. Even the industrial use of steam power is not a new idea. In the first century AD, Hero of Alexandria made a revolving cylinder driven by steam. Hero's cylinder was little more than a toy but, by that time, it was widely known that steam can exert pressure which might be harnessed to do useful work, and cylinders, valves, and other steam-engine components had been designed. Had they been able to produce tougher metals, our ancestors might very well have ushered in 'the age of steam' nearly 2000 years ago!

Of all the water withdrawn from rivers, lakes, and underground sources in the United States today, almost half is supplied to industry and, in Belgium, the figure is more than four-fifths. The quantities involved are impressive — industry takes more than 230 000 cubic kilometres (55 000 cubic miles) of water a year in the United States and almost 7000 cubic kilometres (1700 cubic miles) in Belgium — but misleading because three-quarters of the water taken by industry is used only for raising steam or for cooling. The water is pumped from a nearby source, passed through the factory, and then discharged essentially unaltered. There is an inevitable, very small loss by evaporation but, in a well-designed and carefully managed factory or power station, there is no reason why cooling water should be contaminated chemically.

Of the water that is used industrially other than for cooling, a small amount is incorporated in manufactured products but most is 'process water', used during some stage of manufacturing and then discharged. It is this water that must be treated to remove contaminants. These days, awareness of the need to reduce and eventually to eliminate pollution from this source has led industry to install sophisti-cated monitoring systems that allow scientists to measure precisely the quality of the water discharged so they can detect faulty treatment quickly. In Britain and in many other countries, the result has been a steady improvement in the condition of rivers whose waters are used by industry and consequently a return of wildlife to them. Further advances are possible, and will be made as the necessary technologies become available, but even now it is not unusual for water to be returned to a river in a cleaner condition than it was before it entered the factory!

Discharged cooling water may be warmer than the body of water that receives it. Some years ago this was a cause for concern. It was feared that raising the temperature of the receiving water would be harmful to aquatic organisms, mainly because the amount of dissolved oxygen water can contain decreases as the temperature of the water rises, and many species of insects and fish require high levels of dissolved oxygen. No thrifty manager approves of waste and, whether harmful or not, the heating of a river or lake outside the factory gates is clearly wasteful. Factories began to use their heated cooling water to provide space heating in their own buildings. The 3M (Minnesota Mining and Manufacturing) Company was among the first to

... there is no reason why cooling water should be contaminated chemically.

recycle water in this way in its American factories and then in its European ones. Recycling allows the factory to discharge water at about the same temperature as the receiving water and it also reduces the factory's fuel bills.

Power stations use much more cooling water than most other factories, although most of it is sea water. In some cases, it can be used to provide space and water heating to nearby buildings. The old Battersea Power Station in London used to supply hot water to Pimlico and, at the Drax power station in Yorkshire, 'waste' heat is piped to a greenhouse growing tomatoes, plant nutrients being added to the warm water along the way so that it irrigates the crop and, at the same time, fertilizes it. Much more use could probably be made in Britain and other European countries of such `CHP' (combined heat and power) schemes. In Scandinavia, they account for a significant proportion of domestic heating.

Meanwhile, the slight warming of water is not necessarily harmful. Provided the temperature is not so high as seriously to deoxygenate the water, fish mature faster. When the warm water is fed into a pond, rather than into a river, eels in the pond, for example, can grow to marketable size

in less than two years, rather than their usual eight.

RESERVOIRS, RESERVES, AND RECREATION

As the demand for water has grown, new ways have had to be found to collect and store it in reservoirs. Again, the idea is ancient and techniques for building artificial reservoirs were first developed in Africa and the Near East. In this century, however, the number of reservoirs has increased, the reservoirs themselves have become larger, and, especially in densely populated countries such as Britain, proposals to build new ones understandably encounter vigorous opposition because they involve sacrificing one resource to provide another. A choice has to be made and it is never simple or easy. When plans are made to satisfy a predicted increase in demand for water, several alternative possibilities are examined before the building of new reservoirs is considered. Reservoirs are by no means the first choice. When reservoirs are planned, remote upland sites are preferred to lowland sites, sometimes incorporating a hydroelectric power scheme, mainly to minimize the disturbance to rural communities by choosing more sparsely populated areas.

Even then it is not always possible to avoid controversy, for the chosen area may be highly valued for reasons other than its purely market value. The classic example of such a conflict, described at the time as a choice between flowers and people, occurred in the 1960s at Cow Green in Upper Teesdale. Cow Green lay on the western side of Widdybank Fell, not far from an old lead mine that closed in 1954; a high, remote place, popular with those walkers and climbers who knew of it but of great botanical impor-

Apart from storing water for industrial and domestic use, modern reservoirs also provide habitat, especially for aquatic birds, and a place where local people can walk beside the water. Many allow access for sporting activities.

tance. Upper Teesdale, including the area around Cow Green, contains plant communities that have remained largely unchanged since the end of the last glaciation, about 10 000 years ago — although the flora had not been studied or catalogued thoroughly.

ICI sponsored a full botanical survey of the site ...

Water was needed for the ICI works at Billingham and for a steel works, and the water authority proposed to supply it by building a dam and reservoir at Cow Green. Local opinion tended to favour the scheme, for the factories represented a very substantial development in a region of high unemployment.

The ensuing argument grew very heated but, in the end, it was resolved sensibly, by compromise. ICI sponsored a full botanical survey of the site and the industries concerned postponed their plans

Below: *Cormorants roosting beside a reservoir owned by Thames Water.* Below right: *The raft, on the Farmoor Reservoir, near Oxford, is provided for terns which build their nests on it. By providing large, protected areas of open water, reservoirs attract many birds — and the birdwatchers who study them.*

until the survey was completed. In 1967 the Tees Valley and Cleveland Water Bill authorizing the plan received the Royal Assent and, in due course, the reservoir was filled. Today, Cow Green Reservoir is still there, not far from the Pennine Way, and much of the original Upper Teesdale flora is also still there to be seen, but it is now well documented. As a result of the compromise, the factory was built, but the Upper Teesdale flora now lies inside a national nature reserve, with a nature trail to make it more easily accessible to visitors. What began in conflict ended in greatly improved management of this fragile habitat.

A storage reservoir is nothing more than an artificial lake and, within a few years of its filling, when it has matured sufficiently to blend into its surroundings, it need not be visually intrusive. Wildlife, of course, makes no distinction between a reservoir and any other kind of lake and so, often with a little careful management to assist the process, it can become well stocked with invertebrates and fish that attract human anglers and aquatic birds. The type and extent of the recreational amenities offered by a reservoir obviously depend on its distance from centres of population, but they can be considerable and, in areas where there are no natural

lakes, they can allow people to enjoy activities that previously were not available at all. There are many windsurfers and dinghy sailors whose skills were acquired on reservoirs.

The water contained in a reservoir can provide a valuable amenity, but it is important to prevent its contamination. For this reason there are usually restrictions on the use of the surrounding land. At one time, this aim of protecting water by isolating it meant the public, too, was excluded, but this has ceased to be so as more advanced treatment methods have simplified and reduced the cost of removing such minor pollutants as recreational land use might introduce.

Dinghy sailors can enjoy learning to handle their craft on reservoirs close to home. Experience gained here will be valuable when they sail in tidal waters or on the sea.

If water is essential for life, sometimes it can bring death. The bacteria that may contaminate water include those that cause a range of diseases, including typhus and cholera. Britain, for example, suffered repeated epidemics of both in the eighteenth and nineteenth centuries. In 1849 more than 50 000 people died from cholera in England. The major improvement in public health that marked the latter part of the nineteenth and early twentieth centuries was due very largely to the provision of a public supply of clean, bacterially uncontaminated water. Today,

although there is still concern about some aspects of water quality, an outbreak of disease caused by bacterial contamination would be considered an outrage in any industrialized country.

The Benjamin Sheares Bridge, linking the mainland of Singapore with the islands that have been made by reclaiming land from the sea.

RECLAIMING LAND

There are some parts of the world where the need is not for more water but for more land, sometimes for farming and sometimes for urban development. Swamps and marshes have been drained extensively but it is also possible to reclaim land from the sea. In Singapore, more than 800 hectares (2000 acres) in the Kallang basin, on the southern side of the city, have been made available in this way for housing and for light industry, but the largest and best-known example is to be found in The Netherlands where about 40 per cent of the land area lies below sea-level. The dykes were built initially to prevent coastal erosion but certainly, by the tenth century, they were being used to exclude the sea and river floods from what then became fields, called 'polders', of fertile arable land. The windmills for which the country is famous are used mainly to pump surplus rainwater from the polders.

When land is reclaimed from the sea and covered with buildings or converted into arable fields, the effect on wildlife can be serious. The sea in such places is very shallow and, at low tide, much of the area may be exposed as sand banks, mudflats, and salt marsh interspersed with pools. Mudflats are usually rich in invertebrate life and so provide valuable feeding grounds for wading birds which often congregate in vast numbers on the larger expanses. Sand banks may provide resting places for seals, and, apart from their plant life, salt marshes provide shelter for other aquatic birds. The significance of this loss of habitat is now recognized, and threatened areas are sometimes afforded protection. In New Jersey, for example, a 4000-hectare (10 000-acre) nature reserve has

Holland is famous for its windmills. They are used not to grind corn but to pump surplus water away from the reclaimed land. These windmills are at Zaanse Schaus.

been established along the coast; and, in The Netherlands, the future of the Wadden Zee has been assured so it will remain a sanctuary for the many species that use it. The Wadden Zee, almost enclosed by the Friesian Islands to the north and to the south by the Afsluitdijk, the dam built in 1932 that separates it from the Zuider Zee, is the largest area of coastal wetland in Europe and, over the years, several schemes had been proposed to drain and develop it

These days it is quite usual for industrial companies to participate with conservation and amenity organizations in collaborative schemes, some of which are directly concerned with the provision or improvement of aquatic habitats. The 1970s 'Save the Village Pond' campaign, organized by the British Waterfowl Association and the Ford Motor Company, was widely acclaimed and, in Northumberland, the Druridge Bay complex includes a country park and several nature reserves along a 10-kilometre (6-mile) stretch of coast in what used to be a coal-mining area. Developed jointly by the Northumberland Wildlife Trust, Alcan Farms Limited, and British Coal Opencast Executive, the area provides sand-dunes of considerable botanical interest and, behind the dunes, there are lakes and pools, with reedbeds and five large islands, that attract many species of birds.

The condition of the environment affects us all, whether we work in industry or not, and all of us use the products of industry. The people who work in industry are as likely as anyone else to be concerned about the conservation of landscape and wildlife and they are well aware that industry uses large amounts of water and affects many habitats. They are no more prepared than anyone else to tolerate conflicts between what they do during their working hours and their leisure activities if such conflicts can be avoided. These days, in most cases, they can be.

Florida Everglades

The Everglades, in southern Florida, cover more than 700 000 hectares (17 780 000 acres) in a strip almost surrounding Lake Okeechobee, bounded by mangrove swamp to the south and swamp to the west. Flooded for most of the year, it is a land mostly of marshes, with few trees. The soil is fertile and, since the latter part of the nineteenth century, there have been many schemes to drain the whole area but, although about a tenth had been converted to agricultural use by the 1940s and more recent schemes have increased the farmed area, the operation proved difficult and costly.

The Everglades National Park, covering more than 550 000 hectares (13 970 000 acres), was established first in 1915 and, in its modern form, in 1947, and it is now recognized that, while agriculture is difficult, the wildlife is of international importance. Apart from reserves, a number of sites are set aside for public recreation. Indeed, so great is the scientific and amenity value of the Everglades that their overall size is now being increased by re-flooding areas that were drained in the past.

The great white egret, 90-120 centimetres (35-47 inches) tall, may stalk its prey slowly or stand and wait for food to approach.

The roseate spoonbill is one of the most beautiful birds of the New World tropics.

PLANTS AND ANIMALS OF THE EVERGLADES

The plant life includes eight species of palms, strangler figs, bald cypress, and Madeira mahogany. Alligators inhabit the fresh waters and, near the coast, there are manatees, members of the family Sirenia, which comprises the only herbivorous aquatic mammals. Manatees are social animals that live in family groups and sometimes come together to form herds. Because they will eat vegetation of any kind, it has been suggested that they be employed to graze navigable waterways and so keep them clear of weeds. The snakes include the rattlesnake, water moccasin, coral, tree, and king, there are anole lizards — the New World equivalents of chameleons but much quicker at changing colour — and, apart from the opossum, raccoon, and black bear, the Everglades also have pumas, known locally as 'Florida panthers'.

It is the rich bird life that attracts most interest, however, for the Everglades provide habitat for many attractive species, some of which, like the Everglade kite, are rare. There are also herons, ibises, bitterns, frigate birds, anhingas, gallinules, and eagles. Egrets and roseate spoonbills were brought almost to extinction in the area early in this century because of the demand for their feathers, used in the millinery trade, but they have now recovered, thanks largely to public campaigns, although all the species of the Everglades are constantly at risk from drought, fire, and flood.

The natural landscapes, flora, and fauna of the Everglades are more valuable to naturalists and to visitors in search of recreation than the drained land could ever be for agriculture. With careful management that does not alter their essential characteristics, we may hope they will now survive to delight and enrich people for many years to come.

CHAPTER 2
THE NEED FOR FOOD

Prairie dogs, which are small North American rodents and not dogs at all, live in large communities. Many entrances lead below ground to a complex network of tunnels and chambers sometimes called 'cities'. Over quite a large area outside the city, the animals clear away tree seedlings and woody shrubs that might obscure the view of their sentinels, standing on earth mounds, on whose constant look-out for predators the safety of the colony depends. At the same time, by clearing away woody plants, the animals encourage the growth of the softer plants they prefer to eat. They are managing the landscape around themselves, modifying their environment to their own advantage and, in relation to their size, they are doing so on an impressive scale.

All living things modify their surroundings. Herds of large animals that graze on the great grasslands of the world trample and nibble seedlings and so prevent the

The black-tailed prairie dog (Cyonomys ludovicianus) *clears away plants that would obstruct its view, so encouraging the plants on which it feeds and greatly altering its immediate surroundings.*

growth of trees that, in time, might turn their pastures into forest. Beavers, of course, are famous as builders of dams to create the artificial lakes where they

All living things modify their surroundings.

construct the 'lodges' in which they live.

Humans are no exception to the general rule. We also modify our surroundings to provide ourselves with more space and more food. The extent to which we do so sometimes attracts criticism, but only a profound ignorance of ecology could allow anyone to suppose our behaviour is in any sense unique.

Just like any other species, we have been modifying our environment throughout the whole of our evolutionary history. Before animals and plants were domesticated, our ancestors obtained their food, as some people still do, by gathering wild plants and augmenting this mainly vegetarian diet by fishing, hunting, and, perhaps more commonly, scavenging. Even these apparently innocuous activities sometimes produced significant effects. It is possible that fires, lit deliberately and repeatedly to drive game, contributed to the expansion of the subtropical savanna, pampas, and prairie grasslands of Africa and the Americas and, although the issue is still not resolved, many scientists believe primitive hunting contributed to the extinctions of large numbers of herbivorous mammals in most parts of the world. Entire herds of game were sometimes killed by being driven over cliffs, the tribe then taking as much meat as could be carried and leaving the remainder.

A herd of wildebeest and zebras on the savanna grasslands of Kenya. Humans may have helped create the savanna.

It is also possible, though not certain, that the first farmers were responsible for the 'elm decline' about 5000 years ago. At that time, most of Europe was forested and elm was common. In Ireland and southern England it was the commonest tree. Then, over a period of about 500 years, the number of elms was halved. It may be that farmers cleared areas of forest to encourage grasses which were then grazed intensively, or that they cut fresh leaves to feed their livestock. This might not have killed the trees but it may have reduced their production of pollen which is the main source of our knowledge of plant communities of the past. One way or another, it is likely that the farmers wrought a major change in the composi-tion of the forest. Later they cleared away most of the forest to provide land for their crops. Throughout history, and everywhere in the world, it is the need for farmland that has led to the clearance of forests. In Britain, which was a major exporter of agricultural produce to impe-rial Rome, most of the original forest had disappeared by the time of the Norman invasion in 1066.

FARMING TODAY AND YESTERDAY

Like anyone else, farmers do their best to respond to the demands made on them. Where there is ample land and few mouths to feed, agriculture can be rather more relaxed than it is where the pressure of population requires that output be increased. In many parts of the temperate world, the earliest farming employed a 'slash-and-burn' technology that is used to this day in parts of the tropics. The farmers fell all the large trees in a particular area, where possible choosing sloping ground so that trees can be made to fall down-slope and bring others down with them. The trees are left to wilt and then they and the remaining vegetation are burned. Burning kills growing herbs, destroys some seeds, and the ashes fertilize the soil. Crop seeds are sown in the ashes. The land is farmed for a few years, until yields begin to fall and tree seedlings are establishing themselves once more. At this point, the farmers move to a fresh area, start all over again, and the original area is left to recover. By moving from

The pampas cover about 760 000 square kilometres (293 436 square miles) of Argentina. Above: Pampas comes from a Quechua word meaning 'flat surface' and, in most places, that is what it is, as here in Patagonia in the south. Below: These Urueu-wau-wau Indians still live on the grassland by hunting game. Right: Slash-and-burn clearance of tropical forest, in Colombia.

area to area so that each is visited every fifteen years or so, the farming can be sustained more or less indefinitely and it calls for the minimum of labour, with almost no cultivation of the ground. It becomes exploitive, as it is now in parts of the tropics, when it is called upon to feed more than a small, scattered population, and more farmers must work the land, returning to each site after shorter and shorter intervals.

The form of more sophisticated farming is determined primarily by the topography of the land, the type of soil, and most of all by the climate. Cereal crops, for example, require a minimum amount of warm sunshine to ripen and dry weather for harvesting. A mild, humid climate is

more suitable to growing pasture grasses to feed cattle and sheep. Steep hillsides, high ground, and thin soils may be capable of growing only poor grasses, and the raising of hardy breeds of sheep or goats may be the only kind of farming possible.

It is the type of farming and the technology available to the farmer that give the countryside its overall appearance. This becomes most clearly evident where traces can be found of farming landscapes from the past. In Celtic times, for example, the light ploughs that were used barely scratched the soil and fields were ploughed first in one direction then a second time at right angles. The technique produced small, square fields. In Saxon times a much heavier plough was introduced. Only one ploughing was required, and fields became long, narrow strips. In the eighteenth century, the four-course rotation was introduced to England from continental Europe. It included root crops to supply feed for livestock through the winter — until then many animals were killed in the course of the winter because the supply of hay was insufficient — and because agriculture still required the labour of large numbers of horses, they had to be given priority. This process integrated livestock and arable farming in a system that called for the enclosing with hedges of land that had formerly been open, often to make rectangular fields with neat, straight edges. The enclosures had profound social consequences and aroused bitter opposition.

AN AGRICULTURAL REVOLUTION

Justus von Liebig was one of the most eminent organic chemists of middle of the nineteenth century. The modern 'agricultural revolution' derives very largely from his work, or at least from work that he claimed as his own for his was a somewhat overbearing personality and he was very famous! Von Liebig showed that different plants had different chemical compositions and that the availability of particular chemical elements was critically important

In medieval times, each farming family was allotted a strip of land to cultivate. Because of the way the strips were ploughed, a ridge formed along the boundary between adjacent strips and, in some places, these ridges can still be seen. There are a few places, as here at Combe de Savoie, in France, where land is farmed in strips to the present day, allowing us a glimpse of a once-common landscape.

to plant growth. He argued that a shortage of any one of these elements would impose a limit on the size and number of the plants that required it. The nutrient elements having been identified, it became possible to produce compounds containing them and so to augment deficiencies in soils. 'Artificial fertilizers' had been invented, at least in principle.

Today, organic farmers prefer not to use factory-produced fertilizers and find ready markets for their produce, but the great majority of farmers in the industrialized countries use fertilizers. The elements plants require in the largest amounts are nitrogen, phosphorus, and potassium, and of these, it is nitrogen that most fertilizers supply in the largest amounts. The traditional alternative source of nitrogen is cattle manure and, as the use of modern fertilizers increased, the essential link between crop and livestock farming was weakened. It became possible for farms to specialize, growing only plant crops where the soil and climate permitted. The food they produced could be transported to

Mixed farming tends to produce small fields bounded by hedges strong enough to contain the livestock. This typical mixed-farming landscape is in North Yorkshire.

wherever it was needed to feed animals. Livestock and arable farming both prospered, but increasingly on separate farms.

Inevitably, in Britain but also in many other parts of Europe and in the United States, this led to major changes in the appearance of those parts of the countryside where mixed livestock and arable farmers sold off their animals and began to produce only plant crops. Bigger machines were introduced that could perform routine farming operations faster, so making it possible to cultivate the land

> *... areas on farms are often set aside to develop as wildlife habitat.*

when the soil was neither too wet nor too dry and harvest crops when they were in peak condition. Bigger machines needed more room to manoeuvre; there was no longer any need to contain livestock, and so hedges were removed to make much larger fields. Without livestock, there was no need for pasture, and grassland was ploughed up to make way for more arable crops. Where farmers concentrated on raising livestock, many old pastures were ploughed and reseeded with more nutritious grasses whose growth was stimulated by the use of fertilizers. This loss of semi-natural habitat had an adverse effect on wildlife, most severe in the exclusively arable regions but, in recent years, conservationists, farmers, and the chemical industry have started to collaborate in remedying the situation, for example, in the Farming and Wildlife Advisory Groups. These days, areas on farms are often set aside to develop as wildlife habitat. The Cereals and Gamebirds Research Project, established in Britain in 1983 by members of the Game Conservancy and supported by ICI, has persuaded many farmers to leave untouched the small strip of land, the 'headland',

surrounding each arable field. Such headlands are soon colonized by a wide range of plant and animal species.

When old grassland is ploughed, nitrate stored in the soil is released and some of it drains down through the soil to enter the groundwater from where, years later, it may feed into rivers. This, combined with fertilizer nitrate leaching from cultivated land, has increased the nitrate content of waters in some areas. There are plans to modify farming practices in the affected areas in ways that will reduce the amount of nitrate entering rivers.

Above: *On the flat prairies of North America, fields are very large and the machines that work in them operate in teams. These combine harvesters are cutting wheat in Montana. Below: Around every field there is a narrow strip of land that is not cultivated because it is where the plough turns. Farmers often leave these strips undisturbed to allow wildlife to thrive.*

A NEW GENERATION OF PESTICIDES

It was during World War 2 that DDT was introduced as the first of the organo-chlorines, heralding a new generation of insecticides. Used to control insects that transmit diseases to humans, DDT saved millions of lives but, used overconfidently to control farm pests, its chemical stability and solubility in fats allowed it to be concentrated along food chains and it

The Electrodyn sprayer allows farmers to control pests and weeds by applying a little pesticide very precisely. It is cheap for the farmer and minimizes any risk of harm to the environment.

proved harmful to wildlife. Its use is now restricted or forbidden in many countries. DDT, together with most of the organochlorines, has been replaced by further generations of pesticides that do not persist in the environment and that are more selective in the species they harm.

Five to ten years can elapse between the time a chemical compound is identified as a possible pesticide and the time it is marketed. It takes this long for the potential product to pass through a long series of

... *DDT saved millions of lives* ...

tests, many of which are concerned with its environmental effects. The information obtained from the wildlife surveys and censuses that have to be made before the effect of any product can be assessed are of great value to ecologists. Scientists must discover precisely what happens to any substance once it enters the soil, air,

and water, and the tests are not confined to the country in which it is being developed. Field trials are conducted under the conditions in which the product will be used. ICI, for example, has field stations doing this work in France, Spain, Japan, Malaysia, the Philippines, and the United States, as well as in Britain. Testing ends when the product is marketed, but monitoring continues and any report of unintended damage is investigated.

In addition to testing products, the major manufacturers run training schemes in pesticide handling and use for agricultural extension workers who will then train farm workers in their own countries. By 1986, Shell had trained about 130 extension workers from twenty-six countries.

The second aspect of testing concerns the fate of pesticides in the crop itself. The field stations sample all the crops with which a product may be sprayed. Where the sprayed crop is fed to livestock, the livestock products are sampled. The samples are then analysed by methods

... major manufacturers run training schemes in pesticide handling ...

capable of detecting one part of pesticide in 100 million parts of the sample — the equivalent of detecting one grain of salt in 100 kilograms (220 pounds) of potatoes, and a level far below that which could harm any human or non-human consumer. The maximum levels of pesticide residues considered acceptable in food are set internationally by the United Nations Food and Agriculture Organization and the World Health Organization at one-hundredth the amount that toxicologists find causes no observable effect on health.

In all the industrialized countries, the chemical industry now makes an essential contribution to food production and it is easy to underestimate the size of that contribution. In 1939, faced with the real possibility of a blockade of all sea ports, Britain imported about 70 per cent of all its food. Today, Britain is largely self-sufficient in those foods that can be produced in its temperate climate. If Britain produced as much wheat as it does today using the farming methods of 1945, the area growing wheat would have to increase from 2 million to an impossible 5 million hectares (from 5 to 12.5 million acres).

THE 'GREEN REVOLUTION'

The industrialized countries were the first to benefit from this increased agricultural output, but research programmes to develop improved varieties of maize and wheat began in 1943 in Mexico, and to develop improved varieties of rice in the 1960s in the Philippines. These programmes led to the 'green revolution' in many of the less-developed countries, where the new varieties of staple foods were introduced together with the ancillary technologies needed to grow them. By 1977, the new wheats were being grown on nearly half the total wheat-growing area in developing countries and, between 1966 and 1979, Indian wheat production tripled. Rice yields in some regions have increased eight-fold.

Once food has been produced, it must be transported to urban areas where the human population is concentrated — a long way from the farms. The export and import of food, involving its transport across oceans, form a vital part of world trade. The introduction of refrigeration in ships, starting in 1880 when the *Strathleven* carried the first refrigerated cargo, allowed Australian and New Zealand meat and dairy produce to be marketed in Europe. Since then, new ways of preserving perishable foods, by freeze-drying and

Modern food processing brings us seasonal vegetables throughout the year with very little nutrient loss. These are dwarf French beans being frozen after blanching.

Fishermen on the River Li, in Kwangsi Province, China, using trained cormorants. The birds dive in pursuit of fish which the men then take from them.

storing under strictly controlled conditions of temperature and humidity, for example, have been introduced by the food industry, as opposed to the agricultural industries, while the chemical industry has made it possible to minimize losses in storage due to pests.

FOOD FROM FISH

Although most of our food comes from farms, fish forms an important item in the diet of most countries, but it is only in modern times that people living in cities far inland have been able to eat fresh sea fish. Fish deteriorates rapidly — the original reason for frying it in batter was to disguise the fact that the fish was no

longer fresh — and, until the railways provided rapid transport, people who lived far from the coast ate only freshwater fish or sea fish that had been salted or smoked. The railways brought fresh fish to the cities, and the development of this new market caused a major expansion in the size of fishing fleets.

Fishing is a form of hunting, the most primitive method for obtaining food but,

in modern times, the hunters of the oceans have armed themselves with very sophisticated weapons. Most inshore fleets continue to catch fish with small nets and lines, but even they make use of radar for navigation and sonar for locating their quarry. The larger vessels, working further from their home ports, use similar hunting technologies but their catching equipment, of large drift and purse seine nets, allows them to take an entire shoal at a single haul. Quotas and other restrictions have had to be imposed to prevent the overfishing that can lead to the severe depletion of stocks.

Just as wild mammals were domesticated and became farm livestock, the alternative to hunting fish is to domesticate and then to farm them. Most of the trout and some of the salmon marketed today comes from fish farms, but the idea of farming fish is far from new. In the Middle Ages European monks raised freshwater species in ponds, and wet-rice farmers in Asia have done so for many centuries. But fish are also raised in estuaries and sea lochs or fjords, in brackish water, and, if the cost of fishing were to rise, the farming of marine species might become economically feasible. A range of species has been bred and grown to marketable size experimentally including sea bass, turbot, lemon sole, Dover sole, plaice, and even mackerel.

We think of fish as food for humans, or perhaps as fishmeal to be fed to livestock, but some species also provide useful byproducts. The pharmaceutical industry has extracted and concentrated cod liver oil and halibut liver oil, for example, and, in years to come, krill may turn out to be

Krill (Euphausia superba) *is the abundant shrimp-like animal that forms the base of the Antarctic food chain. Some are processed for human consumption and their shells contain valuable chemicals.*

an even more valuable source of pharmaceutical products.

The word 'krill' comes from the Norwegian *kril*, meaning 'tiny fish', and krill are shrimp-like crustaceans the largest of which grows to a length of about 6 centimetres ($2^1/_2$ inches). They occur in large, dense swarms in Antarctic waters where they are food for many animals, including the baleen whales. As whale numbers have fallen, so krill stocks have increased, together with the populations of many of the animals that eat them. Krill are caught commercially, mainly for human consumption, but processing them is difficult. They deteriorate even more rapidly than bony fish so they have to be processed at sea. They cannot be dried, frozen, or stored in water, however, because they are physically delicate and the proteins in their bodies are soluble in water, and their shells contain unacceptably large amounts of fluoride. The krill are shelled rapidly and usually made into a paste, but the shells may be potentially of more use than the flesh. They contain chitin which can be converted into chitosan, two chemicals that could have great potential. They form stable compounds with heavy metals and coagulate proteins, so they might be used in the purification of water. They also slow the flow of blood from wounds and promote healing; they may have other therapeutic properties

Much of our salmon, and almost all our trout, are produced on fish farms. The men here are feeding salmon smolts, held in cages in sea water in Uyea Sound, Shetland.

and, because they are biodegradable, it may be possible to make containers from them. Much more must be learned about the biology of krill, however, before it is possible to calculate the quantity that may be caught without depleting the stock.

NEW KINDS OF FOOD

The search continues ceaselessly for new sources of food and new ways to make traditional foods more palatable. Soya beans were introduced to North America in the last century but, in Asia, they have been grown since ancient times. Their oil has industrial as well as culinary uses but the beans themselves are of particular nutritional value because they are one of the very few plant products that contains the full range of amino acids the human body requires to make its proteins. Their nutritional quality makes it possible to process soya into a 'meat extender', a product with the same food value as meat that can be used to replace some of the meat in certain products and dishes. Soya protein can also be given an approximately meat-like texture and flavour. In this form it is marketed as 'textured vegetable protein' or 'TVP' and is the basis of 'TV dinners' which have nothing to do with television! Wheat protein can also be processed in this way, and protein can be obtained from even more exotic sources.

Some years ago a considerable amount of research was devoted to the culturing of single-celled organisms, usually yeasts, from which protein was then extracted for use in livestock feed. The advantage was that the raw material could be the wastes from other processes. Hydrocarbon fractions from the petroleum industry were used, as were wastes from the timber industry, from abattoirs, and even from sewage. The technique worked but, in the end, it proved uneconomical and you may be relieved to hear it was abandoned.

It has even been suggested that earth-

Direct drilling of soya beans in Brazil. Soya protein contains all the amino acids needed by the human body. Originally from Asia, soya is now grown in warm climates throughout the world.

worms be exploited for human food because their bodies contain a high proportion of protein in relation to fat. It may sound outrageous, yet every day we consume foods that were once novel. Margarine is the most famous example, invented in the 1860s by the French chemist Hippolyte Mége-Mouriès and made to a formula that has been greatly improved since he launched his highly popular product; and the milk substitutes we add to our coffee owe nothing to the cow except the original idea. These days there is no technical difficulty in converting grass and other herbs directly into a substance virtually indistinguishable from milk.

Agriculture may be regarded as an industry, at least in some senses but, in modern times, more conventional industries have wrought fundamental changes throughout all the pathways that lead from the field to the table. The task now is to transfer these industrial products and techniques to those parts of the world where food is still in short supply and to do so while protecting or enhancing the quality of the environments into which they are introduced.

Farming types

SLASH AND BURN

Where the density of the human population is low, food may be produced by the most ancient of all farming methods, 'slash-and-burn'. Trees and tall shrubs are felled, often in such a way as to bring down others as they fall. They are left for a time for their leaves to wilt; such wood as is needed is removed, and the area is set on fire. The fire removes all vegetation, kills some seeds, and adds ash, rich in potassium, to fertilize the soil. Crops are sown in the cleared ground. These include all the plants needed for food that cannot be gathered more easily in the wild, and usually they are sown all together and not in separate plots. As each crop is harvested, a fresh one is sown until the soil is exhausted, yields fall, and weeds and re-emerging tree seedlings choke and shade the plot. Then the farmers move to a new area and start again. The cultivated area is moved from place to place in a rotation that brings it back to its starting place every twelve to fifteen years, by which time the land has regained its fertility.

Slash-and-burn farming can be sustained indefinitely provided the number of people to be fed remains constant. If the population increases, output can be increased to match only by cultivating more areas. This is not usually possible because neighbouring groups of people are also seeking new areas to feed their increased numbers. The rotation proceeds more rapidly and eventually all the sites become depleted and useless.

FARMING IN NORTH AMERICA

On the grassland plains of North America, the climate is typically continental, with hot dry summers and very cold winters. Cereals, especially wheat and maize which are members of the grass family, grow well. Fields are large, bounded by roads rather than by hedges and, at intervals, the land is left fallow to increase the amount of water stored in the soil. Yields per hectare are much lower than those attained in Europe but the cultivated area is so large that North American farmers produce far more than their own populations require. Agricultural products are among the most important of North American exports.

Where the climate is too dry or the terrain too broken and rocky to permit crop growing, the land may be used for ranching. Large herds of cattle and, to a lesser extent, sheep, are allowed to wander at will over an area that seems vast by European standards, finding food and water as best they may. At intervals, they are rounded up to be counted, checked for disease, some to be sold, and calves to be marked so their owner can be identified.

MIXED FARMING

In western Europe, where the population density is much higher and the climate is of a milder and more humid

A cattle feedlot in Wyoming, where the animals are kept permanently in enclosures and fed a nutritious diet.

Where hillsides are too steep to be cultivated, and their soils too thin and acid, sheep can thrive on the tough grasses and heather.

maritime type, lowland farming is more intensive. Farms are small compared with those of North America and, in most of Europe, they are more likely to be engaged in some kind of rotational mixed farming. Fields are not left fallow, but different crops are grown in each field at different times. In the 'classic' four-year rotation in Britain, each field grew a root crop for livestock feed, originally well fertilized with animal manure, then barley, for livestock feed or for malting to make beer, undersown with grass, then grass, and finally wheat. Most farms would have had some fields growing only grass for grazing or for harvesting to make hay. Since about 1950, this pattern has given way in some places to more extreme systems that grow the same crop, usually barley, year after year and, in others, to new rotations that include such crops as field beans for livestock feed and oilseed rape, grown for its oil. Elsewhere old grassland has given way to 'leys' — temporary pastures composed of only one or two species of grass chosen for their palatability and nutritional value to grazing animals.

In the uplands, where the climate is harsher and the soils poorer, farms tend to be larger but more limited. Beef cattle may be raised on the better

Fertile land is scarce in Japan. Farms are very small and are worked intensively. This worker is hoeing his plot by hand.

land, but elsewhere the principle crop is sheep, born in the hills but often to be sold for fattening on the lowland farms.

INTENSIVE METHODS IN JAPAN

In Japan, there are about 325 people for every square kilometre (840 per square mile) and, because the country is mountainous, only about 16 per cent of the land area is suitable for growing arable crops. Even that land is not very fertile. Consequently, Japanese agriculture is per-

haps the most intensive in the world. The average farm is about 1 hectare (2^1/$_2$ acres) in area, though many are smaller. It may be terraced to prevent the erosion of soil on sloping ground, irrigated, and the farmer will rely heavily on fertilizers and pesticides. Farms are highly mechanized, using machines such as garden tractors whose scale is appropriate to the size of fields. The staple food is rice, in which the country is more or less self-sufficient, and the farms also produce vegetables, fruit, and nowadays many produce beef.

CHAPTER 3
THE NEED FOR CLOTHING

When the fifty-oared galley *Argo* sailed from Thessaly to Colchis under the command of Jason, the mission was to recover the golden fleece of the ram on which Phrixus, Jason's cousin, had escaped his stepmother's attempt to have him sacrificed. The stepmother, Ino, had contrived a harvest failure and said only this sacrifice could avert famine. The ancient story of Jason, the Argonauts, and the golden fleece seems to have economic implications. Some people believe it records the opening up of trade routes to the east. But what was the golden fleece? Did it really exist? If so, was it literally golden because it was used to pan for gold as some have suggested, or was it only metaphorically golden, the source of great potential wealth?

THE WOOL TRADE

Colchis lay to the east of the Black Sea, the region where sheep are most likely to have been first domesticated, perhaps as long ago as 7000 BC. They were valued initially for their milk and meat but domestication brought physical changes,

In Lavenham, Suffolk, the impressive fifteenth-century church is a reminder of the wealth once generated by the wool trade.

one of which has altered the course of history more than once. Wild sheep have a coat of long, stiff hairs over a short-haired, woolly coat that grows only in winter and is moulted in spring. A consequence of domestication was the loss of the bristly outer coat and the development of the woolly undercoat which came to be retained throughout the year. Domesticated sheep have fleeces that can be shorn and then spun and woven into cloth; wild sheep do not. Were the Argonauts really seeking domesticated sheep to form the breeding nucleus of a flock to supply the raw material for a new and extremely profitable industry that would revive the flagging agricultural economy of Thessaly? One way or another, knowledge of how to produce and process wool had reached Greece by the time of Homer, when most Greek clothes were made from wool, and felt was used for the lining of the helmets worn by Greek soldiers.

By classical times the woollen industry was firmly established and it has remained so ever since. Wealthy Romans wore woollen togas, thick and warm in winter, lighter in summer, and the breastplates of Roman soldiers were made from felted wool. A thousand years later the Vikings

---

By classical times the woollen industry was firmly established ...

---

carried woollen cloth to barter for furs in North America. Charlemagne is said to have worn woollen clothes in preference to Byzantine silk. It was the expansion of the wool trade that stimulated the economic growth and urbanization of Europe in the Middle Ages and, in the twelfth and thirteenth centuries in Flanders, that expansion led to the first industrialization of an economy, in the sense we understand the term today.

Sheep-shearing in New Zealand, where itinerant shearers travel from farm to farm. It is skilled, but gruelling work.

The farming of sheep brought prosperity to landowners and the processing of fleeces into cloth and, later, the international trade in woollen cloth financed the growth of cities in western Europe. Until late in the eighteenth century, wool was the basis of by far the most important industry in England and, as recently as the 1960s, Britain was the world's largest exporter of woollen goods.

THE INDUSTRIAL REVOLUTION ON A COTTON THREAD

It was not wool that provided the basis for the Industrial Revolution, however, but cotton, and the mechanization of its processing. This began around the middle of the eighteenth century, but the woollen industry was not affected by it until nearly a century later. Cotton cloth was no more a novelty than woollen cloth. It was being made in India in 3000 BC and reached North, Central, and South America in prehistoric times. It was not new, but the industrialization of its manufacture was.

In the north-west of England a textile industry based on wool and linen was already well established. Exposed to the

The story of cotton

Cotton is grown on farms in lower latitudes throughout the world — China, the USA, the USSR, India, and Pakistan together accounting for about three-quarters of world production. Altogether the crop probably occupies about 34 million hectares (84 million acres).

For some countries it is an important source of export earnings so that, although the crop occupies land that might otherwise produce food, its sale abroad may help finance economic development. Cotton, part of it as spun yarn, part as finished cloth, and part as raw cotton, is Pakistan's most valuable export and Egypt's second most valuable.

The boll weevil is the most serious of the 500 or so species of insects that attack cotton. It feeds on a boll and effectively destroys it.

Cotton bolls in New Mexico. Each fibre is a single cell. Together they protect the seed.

The plant belongs to the genus *Gossypium*, of which four species are cultivated, each yielding a distinctive type of cotton. All cotton plants produce a luxuriant foliage and large flowers, and the fruit develops over a long period. This makes it attractive to pests and parasites. During its growth, the crop is susceptible to attack by more than 500 species of insect pests, the most serious of which are the various species of boll weevils and bollworms, and by a range of soil pests such as eelworms, as well as viruses, bacteria, and fungi. The chemical control of pests and diseases has reduced losses but these remain serious in some producing countries. Weeding has been largely mechanized but some cotton is still harvested by hand.

The crop consists of the seeds and their protective covering. From the outer layer of the seed, single cells grow outward to form a capsule made of fibres, called a 'boll', in which each strand of fibre is a single cell.

PREPARING THE COTTON

After harvest, the bolls are 'ginned' on the farm to separate the fibres from the seeds. The crop produces roughly twice as much seed as it does fibre, by weight. The seeds can then be sold for crushing, to yield cottonseed oil that is refined and sold for culinary use, and a feed for livestock.

The fibres are then baled and transported to a mill where impurities, such as particles of soil, leaf, and seed, are removed, the fibres are 'picked' to align them and

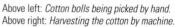
Above left: *Cotton bolls being picked by hand.*
Above right: *Harvesting the cotton by machine.*

make them into a 'lap' rather like a roll of cotton wool. This is 'carded', 'drawn', 'combed', and 'drafted', in a series of operations that convert it into long, progressively finer slivers of aligned fibres, ready for spinning. The preparation of raw cotton is a dry, dusty process that created an unhealthy atmosphere for workers before the introduction of dust-extraction equipment. Spinning and weaving require a humid atmosphere.

These days much of the crop is processed into finished cloth in the country where the cotton was grown, to add as much value as possible to the product before it is exported.

Once picked, the bolls are made into bales and stacked in the field while they await collection.

weather systems moving eastwards to
Britain, across the Atlantic Ocean and
Irish Sea, the climate is more humid than
that of the country to the east, sheltered
by the Pennine Hills. The humid atmosphere was particularly suited to working
with cotton. The fibres become brittle
when dry, and it was there that new machines were introduced to increase output. In 1733 John Kay invented the flying
shuttle, which speeded up weaving so that
four spinners could no longer keep one
weaver supplied. James Hargreaves's
spinning jenny mechanized spinning; in
1769 Richard Arkwright patented his
water frame, so called because it was
operated by water power, which produced
a more tightly spun yarn for making
warps; and in 1779 Samuel Crompton's
mule took the development a stage

*The machines that made the Industrial Revolution: Hargreaves'
spinning jenny, Crompton's mule jenny, Arkwright's water-frame
spinning machine, and Whitney's cotton gin.*

further by combining the jenny and the
water frame. The power loom was invented by 1785, by the Reverend Edmund Cartwright.

These machines were made from new,
stronger materials, principally iron and
steel, thereby stimulating those industries,
and they required new sources of power,
obtained first from water and then from
steam generated by burning coal. Because
they were large and heavy, and powered

*... by the early 1800s, the
Industrial Revolution had
spread to Belgium, ...*

by big engines, the machines came to be concentrated in specialized buildings. This led to the introduction of the factory system, with the division of labour, and an increasing demand for scientific and technical research that would maintain and accelerate the dynamism that had been attained. The process began in Britain but, by the early 1800s, the Industrial Revolution had spread to Belgium, and by the middle of the century to France. German industry did not become industrialized until the 1870s, after the unification of the country.

European manufacturers imported raw cotton, a tropical crop that has adapted to the warmer temperate regions but will not grow in most of Europe. The most tedious task in preparing cotton for spinning is 'ginning' — the separation of the seeds from the fibres that surround them. Eli Whitney mechanized this process in 1793 with his invention of the hand-operated cotton gin, which he then started producing at a factory in New Haven, Connecticut.

The full-scale industrialization of cotton manufacture provided the model that was followed repeatedly throughout Europe and North America. Modern factories are much quieter, cleaner, healthier places than those from which they are descended, and working and living conditions for those employed in them has improved radically. Yet they owe much to those Lancashire models in which were devised the principles on which they are based.

Nor is it only our industrial methods that were fashioned in those early factories. The conditions they produced gave rise to the movements for reform that sought to redress their injustices and harshness, and that did much to create the social and political attitudes of the twentieth century. The cotton gin, for example, increased the rate of production of raw cotton, removing a constraint to the European cotton industry, and led to an

> *... movement for environmental improvement ... began in the nineteenth century.*

expansion of cotton growing in the southern United States. The cotton plantations employed slave labour, and their expansion contributed to the events that led to the American Civil War.

Even the movement for environmental improvement, which many people regard as a very recent phenomenon, began in the nineteenth century. Charles Dickens and William Morris were just two of the authors who wrote about the need to reduce the pollution of air and water.

TWO MORE TRADITIONAL FIBRES

The rise of the cotton industry was accompanied by a decline in the processing of cotton's temperate-climate rival, linen. The flax plant, from whose fibres

Flax: after much processing, the fibres of this plant are woven to make linen. The plant is attractive, but difficult to grow because it must be harvested by being pulled from the ground.

linen is made, probably originated in the Mediterranean region and was being cultivated in parts of Europe in prehistoric times, although it is not clear whether it was grown for its fibre or for its edible seeds. It is a versatile fibre that has given us canvas for sails and tarpaulin, the damask weave that yields fine table cloths and napkins, cambric, and lawn for handkerchiefs. Once the fibre is extracted from the plant stems it can be processed using modified cotton-working machin-

The stages in silk production in China.
Above left: Sorting the cocoons within which the larvae are pupating.
Below left: Spinning the silk taken from the cocoons into threads.
Above right: The silk threads, wound together in ropes, being prepared for weaving.
Below right: The loom provides a frame for the embroiderer, who works her design into the silken cloth as it is woven.

ery, but the quality of the fibre is such that the equipment used to spin and weave it was adapted further for the production of cloth from synthetic fibres.

The fourth traditional fibre used in

cloth manufacture, silk, was economically important in China by 2500 BC but it had been made for so long that its origins, like those of wool in the west, are recorded only in legend. Many insects produce a thread from which yarn can be spun but the true silk moth, *Bombyx mori*, has been fully domesticated for at least 3000 years and may well be extinct in the wild. It is by no means certain that the insect could survive without the attention it receives from the humans who culture it.

The cultivation of silk worms (moth larvae) and production of silk spread widely throughout the ancient world, and was introduced into Europe in the Middle Ages. King James I of England (and VI of Scotland) encouraged the industry; Hernán Cortés introduced it to Mexico in the sixteenth century; and Benjamin Franklin sought to establish it in Philadelphia in the first of many attempts to create an American silk industry, all of which failed. Today almost all silk is produced in Asia, more than half of it in China, and about one-third of the total world production is consumed in Japan.

'ARTIFICIAL SILK'

If it was the processing of cotton that triggered the Industrial Revolution it was the luxuriousness of silk that led to developments which undermined the traditional textile industries. Robert Hooke, in the seventeenth century, first suggested the possibility of extruding a quick-setting

---

... *rayon was the first synthetic fibre.*

---

liquid through fine nozzles to imitate the way the silk moth larva produces silk but it was not until 1842 that Louis Schwabe made a machine that would do so. A few years later, in 1846, the Swiss chemist C F Schönbein discovered nitrocellulose, and, in 1855, George Audemars took out the

first patent on equipment for the manufacture of 'artificial silk', the fibre that has been called 'rayon' since 1924 and more recently either 'viscose rayon' or 'acetate'.

Made from cellulose, the principal constituent of the cell walls of plants and the most abundant of all natural organic substances, rayon was the first synthetic fibre. The cellulose is obtained mainly from wood pulp and short cotton fibres (linters). The cellulose can be treated with sodium hydroxide (caustic soda), to produce viscose rayon, the most absorbent of all synthetic fibres, with many uses. It can also be treated with glacial acetic acid (ethanoic acid), acetic (ethanoic) anhydride, and sulphuric acid. The process is called 'acetylation' and it produces cellulose acetate. Cellulose acetate can be used to produce a fabric called 'acetate', which is soft to the touch and stronger than viscose rayon when wet. If the acetylation is carried to completion it yields cellulose triacetate. Triacetate fabrics resist shrinking and stretching, so they keep their shape well. Rayons can also be made into a plastic suitable for injection moulding. Taken together, the world annual production of viscose rayon and acetate for textile use is about 3 million tonnes.

SYNTHETIC TEXTILES

Clearly, this is a major industry, but the rayons comprise only one branch of the synthetic textile industries, and these days it is the smallest. The largest, in terms of output, is polyester, a group that includes 'Dacron' and 'Terylene', of which the world produces about 7.5 million tonnes a year. The total annual world production of all synthetic textile fibres approaches 14 million tonnes. The annual world production of cotton is around 18.5 million tonnes, of wool (after degreasing) 1.8 million tonnes, and of silk 63 000 tonnes, a total of just under 21 million tonnes. Synthetic fibres now supply the material

Versatile, modern fibres are produced from raw materials made in factories like this one, at Wilton, Tees-side, which makes nylon. Such factories release vast areas of land.

for 40 per cent of all our textiles.

Each of the synthetic fibres has its own characteristics. Nylon is tough, elastic, and suitable for making such things as carpets and upholstery in vehicles, as well as underwear. The polyesters can be made crease-resistant or permanently pleated so they are suitable for making trousers and skirts. Acrylic fibres are short and flexible and are used to make sweaters and baby clothes. Synthetic fibres, or non-fibrous materials, can imitate furs, so helping to reduce the demand for furs obtained by hunting mammals, some of which are now endangered, and they can produce passable imitations of leather and suede. If we allow that the keeping of domesticated livestock can be justified, then skins and leather made from skins are by-products available inevitably when the animals die, but synthetic alternatives to such animal products, which are of pleasing appearance and at least as weatherproof and durable as the originals, are nevertheless valuable.

NEW OPPORTUNITIES FOR ALL

In some cases, synthetic fabrics are much better than the natural fabrics they replace. Half a century ago, for example, if you planned to visit the polar regions, you would have to obtain clothing based on furs, lambswool, and wool, with an outer layer probably made from canvas. It would have been heavy, bulky, and restricting. You might also have had to take tents, made from heavy canvas. Today you would be equipped entirely in synthetic fabrics. They would be light, allow full movement for your limbs and fingers, and they would keep you warmer and drier than natural products. Your tent would be made from a lighter material that packs into a smaller space, is much easier to carry, and that affords at least as much protection from wind, rain, and snow. Not many of us can visit polar regions, of course, but most of us benefit from a temperate-climate version of such bad-weather clothing. Modern 'breathable' garments that pack into a small bag when they are not being worn are proof against the worst weather and vastly superior to the garments they have replaced, and it is

New clothes are no longer the unattainable luxury ...

modern lightweight tents that have made back-packing possible.

Apart from the rayons, all the synthetic fibres are made from organic chemicals derived from oil or coal. It is still the traditional textile industry that weaves the fibres into finished fabrics, but the production of the fibres is part of the chemical industry.

New clothes are no longer the unattainable luxury they were for most working people a hundred years ago. The farm and

Climbers and hill walkers can now use tents, made from synthetic fibres, that are more weatherproof and very much lighter than the cotton tents they have rendered largely obsolete.

mill workers who produced raw fibres and textiles throughout the Industrial Revolution and for long afterwards could not afford to wear them. They wore second-hand clothing, and wore it to destruction. Mass production, involving the industrialization of the craft of tailoring, brought new clothes within the economic range of many more people, but it was the widespread introduction of synthetic fibres, which are relatively cheap to produce, that has provided the range of fabrics and styles we now take for granted. The standard of dress and furnishings that is general throughout the industrialized countries today and that is becoming more widespread in the newly industrializing countries would astound a visitor from any period in the past.

THE DYESTUFFS INDUSTRY

Our clothes and furnishing fabrics are available not only in a range of textures and styles that is unprecedented, they are also more brightly coloured. In Germany the Industrial Revolution started late, and

Enjoying the snow with more than a little help from industry! The toboggan is made from plastic, as are the frames and lenses of the sunglasses, and the boots. The suit is of synthetic fibres.

based itself not on textile production but on the manufacture of industrial chemicals, and in particular on dyes.

Until the nineteenth century, almost all dyes were derived from plants, minerals, or in a few cases from animal products. Most of the colours were subdued and few were truly fast. Tyrian purple was made from shellfish, mainly molluscs of the genus *Murex* (*Purpura*, the Latin word for purple, is also the name of a molluscan genus from which purple dye can be extracted). It was very expensive and in Rome it could be worn only by members of the aristocracy, a tradition preserved by the Roman Catholic Church, where priests of the rank of cardinal wear purple. It was not uniquely European, however. The first Europeans to visit Mexico found *Purpura* shellfish were being used to dye cloth. The red tunics of English soldiers were dyed with cochineal, made from the crushed bodies of female insects (*Dactylopius coccus*), native to South America but introduced into Europe. 'Scarlet' originally meant a rich, brightly coloured cloth that was often red but not necessarily so. A red dye can also be obtained from brazilwood trees

We take our synthetic fibres and dyes for granted yet, without them, we would not be able to enjoy the bright colours and pleasing textures that are so much a part of modern living.

(*Caesalpinia* species), obtained first from southern Asia but then discovered in South America. It was so valuable that the country Brazil was named after it because that was its first important export. Its value was not unique, however. Most dyestuffs were highly prized.

Bright colours were a mark of wealth and rank but, during the nineteenth century, chemists all over Europe were busy exploring the compositions of pigments and experimenting with new combinations of compounds. In 1834, it was found that oxidizing aniline, an organic (carbon-containing) compound with many industrial uses, formed a solid that could be used as a colour-fast, intensely black dye; in 1869 the first naturally occurring dye was made synthetically; the first fluorescent dyes were produced in 1871; and, as the discoveries multiplied, the factories making the new dyes became famous. The Badische Anilin und Soda Fabrik (BASF) and Meister, Lucius und Brüning which changed its name to Farbwerke Hoechst are just two of the companies whose prosperity began a century ago with synthetic dyes, as the economy of the newly federated German states became industrialized. Synthetic dyes were so successful that vegetable dyeing died out completely in the industrialized countries.

BIG MAY BE BEAUTIFUL, TOO!

The factories producing synthetic fibres and dyes are often large. They use a range of substances, some of which are very toxic, corrosive, or inflammable. And, at the end of the industrial processes, there are noxious wastes for disposal. While no one pretends that a large factory is pretty, size does confer certain environmental advantages as well as the more obvious economic ones. If you compare one imaginary factory making, say, 1000 tonnes of a particular substance with 100 factories each making 10 tonnes of the same substance in the same time, those advantages become apparent. One factory, however large, occupies a single site and has a limited and known number of points at which it can communicate wastes to the world outside its own gates. A hundred smaller factories occupy 100 separate sites, and each factory has its separate outlets, so the number of places at which wastes may be discharged is multiplied many times. These days, the laws regulating the disposal of industrial wastes are strict, and the cost of monitoring discharges and the policing of regulations inevitably increases in direct proportion to the number of industrial sites. The technology exists to prevent pollution by factories, and large factories are more likely to be able to afford the necessary equipment and staff. In Britain, every year The Environment Foundation sponsors an award for the best examples of pollution abatement technology. Any company or individual may enter the competition but a company that does so must have sufficient resources to be able to conduct the scientific research and technical development needed to produce devices that may not contribute directly to the manufacture of the products it sells. Environmental protection tends to favour the larger organizations.

THE IMPACT OF NATURAL FIBRES

Even so, natural fibres, naturally dyed, may seem to be gentler and safer than those made in large factories. The impression is misleading. Wool, for example, must undergo a considerable amount of processing before it can be spun and, in the past, its preparation was the source of a great deal of river pollution.

The natural fleece is rich in grease, mainly lanolin, secreted by the sheep, together with plant seeds, other scraps of vegetation, and dirt. The wool is 'scoured' (washed) in soft, warm, soapy water, sometimes with the addition of an alcohol to help emulsify the grease; it is then rinsed in clean water. As much as possible of the grease is recovered, although the market for lanolin tends to be over-supplied and so the grease usually remains as waste. Disposing of the dirty water is now difficult. Traditionally, it was discharged into the river from which the scouring water was taken but this is now forbidden. Especially in the United States, a considerable amount of wool is scoured using solvents similar to those employed in dry cleaning. Sulphuric acid and synthetic detergents are often used to help remove plant material from the wool.

The operation used to be seriously polluting, and there is a further hazard to human health. The disease anthrax has several names, one of which is 'wool-sorter's disease' because the handling of fleeces is one of the main routes by which anthrax is transmitted from livestock to humans

The processing of silk causes no serious pollution but the insects themselves are reared under the most intensive system of agriculture ever devised. Cotton and flax are prepared for spinning mechanically, with no need for washing, but their production raises quite different environmental questions. They are grown as farm crops on land that might otherwise be used to produce food. The seeds of both plants are crushed to provide vegetable oils and the residues form a cake used to feed livestock, but much more food could be produced were the farms to grow crops that could be eaten directly by humans. This is of little concern in Europe and North America, where food is plentiful, but in some less-developed countries where hunger is widespread, the wisdom of growing such cash crops is often questioned.

Vegetable dyeing also involved the use of hazardous chemicals. The dyeplants themselves were innocuous, but most can be used only in conjunction with a mordant, a chemical that fixes the dye to make it fast and that often modifies the colour; some mordants are toxic. Cochineal produces a bright scarlet only when it is mordanted with tin, for example, and potassium dichromate was also used widely.

IMPROVING THE QUALITY OF LIFE

All commercial dyeing is now based on synthetic dyes, and synthetic fibres are used to make a large proportion of our fabrics. Between them these two branches of the chemical industry have brought us cheaper, more plentiful, more brightly coloured, and often more comfortable and durable materials. These have contributed greatly to the quality of our lives while liberating agricultural land for other uses, and the factories engaged in their manufacture cause no more pollution, and probably much less, than those they replaced.

BROADENING OPPORTUNITIES

Informal outdoor recreation is now by far the most popular leisure activity in most industrialized countries. The increase in car ownership has made this possible but, to a large extent, it is synthetic fabrics that have made it comfortable and safe.

INTO THE 'GREAT OUTDOORS'

Outdoor clothing that is light, weatherproof, and 'breathable' allows walkers to spend all day in the rain without getting wet or dangerously cold. Back-packers need robust, durable tents that fit into small bags and are light to carry. Today, they are usually made from synthetic materials that are light and repel water so they cannot become sodden.

Transparent fabrics, possible only with synthetics, provide us with tents that have windows and allow windsurfers to see where they are going.

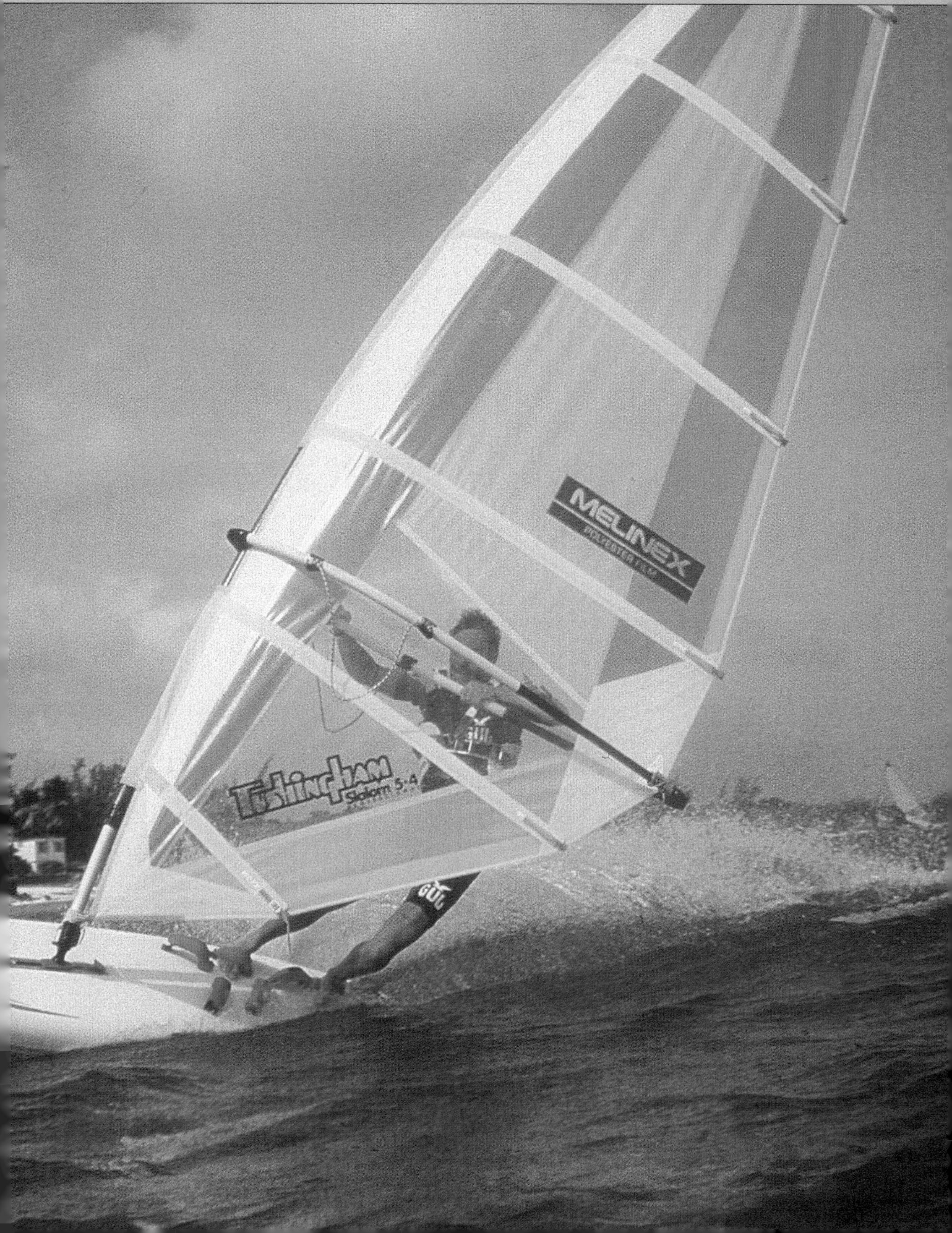
MELINEX
Tushingham
Slalom 5.4

CHAPTER 4
TIMBER

The times in which we live are sometimes called the 'Space Age', the 'Atomic Age', or the 'Computer Age' to contrast them with the Stone, Bronze, and Iron Ages, historical periods that are named for the materials on which their technologies mainly relied. If you look around your own home, however, you will see that, even today, the most widely used material of all has been overlooked. Wood is so common, we use so much of it and always have done, that, unless our attention is caught by a particularly attractive grain or an example of exceptionally skilled craftsmanship, we take it for granted. It becomes invisible. Yet it is wood that supplies the raw material for many ornaments, some kitchen utensils, most of our furniture, most of our floors, and, usually hidden away, the structure of our homes — the roof trusses, joists, and rafters. Remove all the wood from your home and it would look very bare for the short time before the structure collapsed!

The 'Wood Age'

Everybody enjoys a log fire and, for most of history, wood has been the most important fuel. These days wood contributes very little to the total sources of

Below: *At the Korean Folk Village, in Korea, paper is still made the traditional way, from the bark of mulberry trees, one sheet at a time. The finished product is of superb quality, but expensive.* Right: *The great expanse of the South American tropical rainforest in the Amazon Basin, at Roraima, Brazil.*

energy of the industrialized countries but, in other parts of the world, it is still very important. More than one-quarter of all the energy used in South America and about three-quarters of that used in Africa is obtained by burning wood.

We use wood in other ways, too. This book is made from wood that has been

> ### *... wood is one natural resource that perpetually renews itself.*

reduced to a pulp and its fibres reconstituted as paper. So is your daily newspaper, much of the packaging on the goods you buy, and, even in the 'Computer Age', so is the paper used in vast quantities by computer printers. Our demand for wood

seems insatiable but, with sensible management, it can be sustained because wood is one natural resource that perpetually renews itself. Provided the number of trees planted or allowed to regenerate naturally is equal to the number felled, there is no reason to fear the stock will ever be depleted.

That is the theory, but the reality is rather different. Forests occupy land and, throughout history, the principal reason for clearing them has been to use that land to grow farm crops. During the 10 000 or so years since farming began, rather more than 15 per cent of the world's forests and woodlands have been cleared to provide land for agriculture. In

Felled timber, much of it destined for paper-making, is transported by floating it to the mill. These logs are on Lake Saimaa, Finland. Paper and paper products account for almost one-third of all Finnish export earnings.

Modern paper-making at Irvine, Scotland. Pulp, mixed with water, is sprayed on to a blanket on a rotating drum, from which it is lifted as a continuous sheet, pressed, dried, and finally made into these large rolls, called 'webs'.

the temperate regions, especially in Europe, the proportion is much higher. Now it is tropical and subtropical forests that are being cleared, mainly for the same reason, and the clearance creates a vicious spiral, driving those searching for timber and fuel ever deeper into previously undisturbed areas. Much of the timber is exported, and much of the fuel is used, as wood or charcoal, in the rapidly expanding cities, sometimes leaving rural communities with insufficient for their own needs. Where wood is the main fuel and is plentiful, each person may use more than 2.5 tonnes of it a year for cooking and for water and space heating. Where it is in short supply, consumption falls dramatically. In Mali and Niger, for example, where wood is now scarce, people use barely half a tonne a year.

It may seem that, in clearing their forests to provide the land and resources that will enable them to industrialize their economies, the countries of the tropics are doing no more than European countries did many centuries ago. This is only partly true but the European and American experience may be helpful. For one

thing, it led to the introduction of sustainable systems of management and to the fairly recent invention of plantation forestry.

When farmers first began to cultivate the soils of Europe, the lowland areas were blanketed almost completely by forests. The forests had largely disappeared from the Mediterranean region by classical times leaving, in some places, a legacy of soil erosion that shaped the landscapes we now find beautiful. In Britain, too, the clearance of forests allowed an attractive countryside to evolve. The trees that once covered rolling hills of the chalk downlands in southern England were removed in Neolithic times and, to this day, they are prevented from reverting to woodland only by the animals that graze them. The upland heaths lost their forests in the Bronze Age, more than 4000 years ago, were cultivated intermittently over succeeding centuries, grew heathers that

covered by useless trees and set to work at once to clear it. Attitudes changed with the rise of popular interest in natural history, especially in the last century, but our present affection for forests is of very recent origin and we should not be too critical if the peoples of the tropics do not share it.

The demand for fuel for the smelting of metals, especially iron, and for timber to build ships had only a minor effect on British forests. The major expansion in shipping occurred in the first half of the nineteenth century. That is when about half of all the timber ships ever built in Britain were constructed, mainly from home-grown timber — apart from masts which were usually imported — and without placing undue strain on woodland resources.

FUELLING THE REVOLUTION

As it began to expand at the start of the Industrial Revolution, iron smelting stimulated a very ancient form of woodland management. Coppicing may have

Above left: *A conifer plantation forest in Wales. Such plantations are criticized for altering the colour and texture of the landscape but, biologically, they are much richer than* (below) *the deforested and eroded landscapes of Greece.*

were grazed by sheep from medieval times until the last century, and today are reduced by repeated fires and erosion to infertile wastes — but wastes whose scenery attracts millions of visitors every year. Most of the British forest may well have been cleared by the time the Romans departed. The Domesday survey, in 1086, records more woodland than there is today, but little of it is likely to have been original, primary forest.

For most of our history until the last century, forests were regarded by most people as obstacles to be removed, dismal places inhabited by dangerous animals and criminals. Timber was essential, but this did not make people love the ' wildwood'. Think of the way forests are portrayed in our folk tales, as dark, menacing, and the people in them as either exceedingly violent or exceedingly poor. Early settlers in North America found a wasteland

been practised in prehistoric times and was widely established in Europe by the eleventh century. A tree is coppiced by felling it with a cut just above ground level. The stump then produces many stems which grow more or less vertically. When they attain a useful size, these stems are cut to provide thin wood, either to make a wide range of household items or to be processed into charcoal, a fuel that burns at a higher temperature than wood. The stump regenerates its thin stems repeatedly for a very long time. Indeed, somewhat paradoxically, such abuse actually increases the lifespan of many species of trees. Coppiced woodland is harvested on a rotation so that each tree is

Most of Dartmoor has looked like this at least since medieval times. There are wooded areas, but the name 'Dartmoor Forest' probably describes a wasteland area preserved for hunting.

> *... such abuse actually increases the lifespan of many species of trees.*

cut every twelve to fifteen years. Selected trees are usually allowed to grow to their full, 'standard' size to provide timber, mainly for construction, so the full management system is known as 'coppice-with-standards'. Pollarding, in which trees are cut in the same way but about 2 metres (6^1/$_2$ feet) above ground level, produces similar regrowth. Grazing animals cannot be allowed into coppice because they would damage the new growth, but grazing can be combined with pollarding.

PLANTATION FORESTRY

Trees were planted deliberately from very early times but the idea of producing timber from plantations, grown for the purpose, is more recent. The earliest plantation recorded, of conifers, was planted in Nuremberg in 1368; more may have been planted in Scotland in the sixteenth century; and a few, small ones were grown in England during the two succeeeding

centuries. The large expansion in plantation forestry, however, did not take place until the middle of the present century. The Forestry Commission was created in Britain in 1919 to provide a permanent and reliable source of timber, and private landowners were encouraged to follow its example. Today, more than 2 million hectares (5 million acres) of Britain are growing productive woodland, rather more than half of it privately owned. About one-third of the total area is planted to broadleaved trees, the remainder to conifers, and about 2 per cent is managed as coppice.

In the United States, the success of the European settlers in clearing forests was so dramatic that, by the nineteenth century, it was possible to predict the date by which supplies of forest products would be insufficient to meet demand. Such profligacy was challenged, most influentially by George Perkins Marsh (1801-82), for twenty years the United States ambassador to Italy where he saw the consequences of deforestation in the Mediterranean area. The pressures for conservation led to the passing of the

Freshly coppiced hazel, with oak standards. The hazel, here seen cut to the ground, will grow to produce poles that will be cut again in twelve to fifteen years.

Forest Reserve Act in 1891, establishing federal forests that are managed sustainably, and the recognition that forests were a valuable natural resource that was being squandered led to further conservation measures, including the setting aside of large areas of land as national parks, designed to preserve them for public enjoyment and also to protect their natural resources from uncontrolled exploitation. Yellowstone National Park was designated in 1872, Yosemite in 1890, Mount Rainier in 1899, and more have been added since so that now the national parks cover more than 12 million hectares (30 million acres).

PAPER FROM TREES

Fears that the American forests would soon disappear arose principally from a technique that is believed to have been invented in 1863, at a paper mill in Maine. Workers there managed to make wood into a pulp from which paper could be made and, in 1867, a mill in Curtisville, Massachusetts, began mass-producing paper for the first time. Woodpulp paper was so much cheaper than paper made from rags that it rapidly supplanted the traditional product and, in the eyes of early conservationists, the paper mills threatened to devour the forests. Today, of all the wood that is used other than for fuel, more than one-third is made into

Yellowstone National Park, covering almost 900 000 hectares (2.2 million acres) in the western United States, consists mainly of high volcanic plateaus surrounded by mountains. About 90 per cent of it is forested — and there are also fossil forests.

Acid rain

It is more than a century since rainfall downwind of industrial Manchester was found to be abnormally acid, but acid rain did not emerge as an important international issue until the late 1960s. Lakes and, to a lesser extent, trees were found to be suffering damage in southern Scandinavia. In the late 1970s, forests were found to be damaged in West Germany, and later in Central Europe, the north-eastern United States, and south-eastern Canada.

This damage became the subject of intensive scientific research which has shown the cause to be much more complex than was supposed and to vary from one affected area to another. The European drought in 1976 injured forests but symptoms did not appear until some years later. In some places, the choice of forest sites and planting methods led to the acidification of soils. Disease and deficiencies of nutrients also damaged trees. Acid rain was one cause among several.

Despite the name, rain usually runs off leaves and drains quickly from the soil so that, even if it is unusually acidic, it causes little harm to vegetation. Mist is much more damaging, for it coats leaves with a film of moisture so they are in contact with the acid for much longer. Airborne acid particles may also be deposited from dry air.

Industrial emissions of air pollutants over parts of eastern Europe are much higher than those of western Europe and North America.

THE GUILTY SUBSTANCES

Sulphur dioxide, which reacts with other constituents of the air eventually to form sulphuric and other acid, accounted for the increased acidity of clouds and rain in some places. In others, nitrogen oxides, leading to the formation of nitric acid, were the main ingredient, and in some places, strong sunlight driving reactions involving nitrogen oxides and unburned hydrocarbons produced ozone, which is also harmful to plants. Damage is most severe in regions, such as Scandinavia, where soils are developed over rocks that contain little limestone to neutralize acids. In the soil, acids may react to release aluminium compounds that may drain into lakes, where they are harmful to fish.

Damage to German trees is due partly to pollution from vehicle exhausts.

Vehicle exhaust emissions are the main source of nitrogen oxides and ozone, the principal chemical cause of damage in Germany, and they are produced nearby. There is little or no sulphur pollution in German forests. Sulphur dioxide is emitted by industrial processes, principally power generation, that burn fuels containing sulphur, but coal-burning power stations probably account for no more than half of the airborne sulphur reaching southern Scandinavia and eastern North America. Large blooms of marine algae, observed in recent years in most seas, emit dimethyl sulphide, much of which forms particles of sulphate on to which water vapour condenses, dissolving the sulphate to form sulphuric acid. In areas further inland, such as Central Europe, heavy industries in countries with lax pollution controls are the most significant source of acid.

Studies of acid rain demonstrated very clearly that airborne pollutants can cross seas and frontiers, and this led to international agreements to curb gaseous emissions. The installation of desulphurization plant at coal-burning power stations will contribute to a reduction in acid deposition. The more stringent limits on vehicle emissions, now in force in the United States, Japan, and many other industrial countries and soon to be standardized throughout the EEC, will also help.

paper or cardboard. Recycling could reduce this demand, of course. Two Pollution Abatement Awards have been made in connection with paper recycling: one to Kenneth McMillan of Friends of the Earth for forming Waste Paperbanks Limited, a company that planned to organize and distribute wheeled cages to collect waste paper, rather like bottle banks; the other to the Resins and Organics Division of Albright and Wilson for a chemical system to attract and polymerize particles of print which can then be separated. This improves the whiteness of recycled pulp, reducing the need for bleaches and whiteners and, by retaining the ink, it reduces the risk of pollution.

As fast-growing conifer plantations were established in temperate latitudes, partly to satisfy this demand for pulp, the more attractive hardwoods came to be supplied principally from the tropics. The trees were taken from the wild, but logging operations often caused great damage. Natural forest in temperate regions is usually dominated by about ten to fifteen species. Tropical forest, especially in the

Two Pollution Abatement Awards have been made in connection with paper recycling ...

humid tropics, is often, although not everywhere, much more diverse, the extreme example being 1 hectare ($2^1/_2$ acres) of Amazonian forest that was found

The deforestation of steep slopes often leads to extensive erosion as the topsoil is washed away into the valleys, causing the silting of rivers and leaving the hillsides bare and barren. This badly eroded hill country is in India.

to contain 230 species of trees. The trees yielding the most popular woods may occur at the rate of only a dozen or so per hectare (five per acre). Other trees were cleared to make way for logging equipment; the felled trees often brought down others as they dropped, and more damage was caused as the huge trunks were dragged away. A gap was created in the forest so, little by little, the forest became pockmarked with small areas, outlined by access tracks, in which more light-demanding species grew, and the composition of the forest changed. In many places, the removal of large trees and the provision of access allowed people to move in and convert the land to other uses. It happened one small gap at a time but, in aggregate, the effect was severe.

The clearance of European forests also happened in this piecemeal fashion, one small area after another, but more slowly. The number of tree species was smaller, so timber could be obtained closer at hand, and it would have been used locally, for there was no international trade in timber. Yet, in the end, our forefathers removed almost all the original forest.

Coniferous woodland on the edge of the valley and deciduous woodland on the ridges support much wildlife and prevent erosion.

FORESTS FOR FUN

The modern European forests may be commercial plantations, growing trees as crops, but nowadays they supply much more than timber. Forestry is an industry that has learned to welcome the public on to its premises. Forests have become tourist attractions in response to the growing popularity of recreational activities in rural surroundings. In some European countries, especially in Germany, forests are popularly associated with health, and healing properties are attributed to them. Whether they go there for their health or simply for relaxation, visitors to European forests can walk along well-marked paths, routed away from current forestry operations, with leaflets and guidebooks to help them identify tree species and to draw their attention to features of special interest. There are picnic sites, camping and caravan sites with all the facilities the modern camper expects to find, and visitors from the cities now augment significantly the income from forestry.

Interest in conservation has encouraged the planting of mixed woodlands, many of which will develop into broadleaved woodlands when the conifers, planted to provide shelter for the more slow-growing broadleaved seedlings, have been harvested. The design of forests has improved, to give those now being planted softer, more irregular edges that allow them to blend more pleasingly into the landscape.

THE TROPICAL ARK

If temperate forests can be seen to have values, including commercial values, extending far beyond the market price of their timber, this is much truer in the case of tropical forests. Covering roughly 1 billion hectares ($2^1/_2$ billion acres), they are estimated to harbour half of all species of plants and animals.

The plants include many that are used only locally but that, with proper development, could find export markets. In the 1970s the National Academy of Sciences in the United States conducted a survey by sending a written enquiry to plant scientists around the world asking them to list those tropical plants that in their view could be exploited profitably. The scientists replied with a list of 400, from which the Academy panel selected three dozen. Not all grow in forests but many do, yielding fruits, oilseeds, gums and waxes, and the buriti, said to be the most plentiful palm in the world, that might be grown as a crop to provide starch, fruit, fibre, and timber.

In the humid tropics, most forests are fragile because they grow on thin, ancient, exhausted soils, their nutrients held not in the soil, as in temperate forests, but in the vegetation itself. When plants and animals die, they are recycled quickly. When the forest is cleared, the soil is prone to rapid erosion, the leaching of such nutrients they contain and, before long, the land may be reduced to a condition little better than desert.

The scientific and potential commercial value of the tropical forests is now widely recognized, and the threats to them have been identified. Estimates of the rate at which tropical forests are being cleared vary widely but the Food and Agriculture Organization of the United Nations predicts that at the present rate, about 150 million hectares (375 million acres) of the remaining closed-canopy forest and about 76 million hectares (190 million acres) of open woodland will be cleared by the end of the century. The loss is most severe in West Africa.

For many countries in the tropics, the forest occupies land many local people believe could be used more profitably, just as clearing the forests of Europe and the United States led to agricultural and then industrial expansion. At the same time, the forests constitute those countries' most valuable natural resource. Some of the largest industrial companies have responded to these apparently conflicting needs by joining in three-way collaborations with governments in tropical-forest countries and with intergovernmental institutions to promote schemes that will permit the undisturbed forest to be

> *... undisturbed forest to be preserved without compromising economic development.*

preserved without compromising economic development. The overall aim is to halt deforestation and to foster forms of development that do not deplete the resource on which they depend. This involves reforming laws concerning land ownership and tenure to make existing, better quality farm land more widely accessible to peasant farmers while allowing the use of forest land to be more closely regulated. Agreements on logging concessions have to be altered, and the export of logs forbidden and factories installed to add value to timber by converting it into finished goods locally. National parks and reserves have to be designated and timber needs satisfied from plantations rather than from virgin forest.

The International Tropical Forest Action Plan encourages these objectives and the International Tropical Timber Agreement, negotiated under the auspices of the United Nations, was adopted in 1983, ratified in 1985, and came into operation in 1987. It requires signatory governments to impose tariffs on imports of tropical timber, the revenue generated being used to fund sustainable projects in producing countries. The World Bank has started to examine much more critically than it used to do the environmental consequences of projects it is asked to finance.

There are many ways in which industry can help. Obviously, plans for industrial projects should take account of their effect on undisturbed forest. In some cases, it may be possible to locate industries on sites somewhat larger than they need for their own activities to protect the 'surplus' land from development of any kind.

Learning from the experience of their own countries, probably the most practical way to protect virgin forest is to provide an alternative resource in the form of plantation forests. Where the clearance of forest is unavoidable if a project is to proceed at all — as it is, for example, if minerals lying beneath the forest floor are to be mined — the lost forest should be replaced by at least an equivalent area of plantation to sustain the livelihoods of local people who are not employed in the project itself.

Producing a plantation involves much more than ploughing and and planting trees. Sites must be chosen with care, and the trees to be grown with still more care, for the species that grows most easily and

In tropical South America, forest clearance exposes an ancient, inherently infertile soil to alternate baking in intense sunshine and drenching in heavy rain. The consequent erosion is often severe, as here, in Brazil.

quickly may compete too successfully and invade, and eventually take over, the nearby forest. *Eucalyptus* species were among the first to be tried and they proved difficult to contain, although they can be grown satisfactorily on appropriate sites and with good management. Projects must begin with detailed site investigation and must be backed by thorough research by forestry scientists and ecologists.

The ideal site is one where the plantation will retain water and bind soil, for this will reduce soil erosion. At the same time, however, the trees should not be planted where they will use water that is needed for other purposes. Trees take a great deal of water from the ground and evaporate it from their leaves, and fast-growing plantation trees use more than those in the natural forest, which grow more slowly. A plantation should regulate the run-off of water and help protect the catchment.

The natural forest cycles its own nutrients but plantation trees are harvested and removed, not recycled. Unless the nutrients in the trees themselves are returned to the soil in the form of fertilizers, the plantation is doomed to fail within a few years. This is true of any plantation but particularly so in the tropics, where nutrients are stored in the living plants and soils are inherently infertile. Fertilizer must be supplied, or produced in local factories, and ways have to be found to apply it without affecting the surrounding environment. If fertilizer leaches into natural forest it can encourage the growth of more aggressive plant species which, in time, will alter the botanical composition; and it will also have adverse ecological effects if it drains into rivers.

Pesticides, too, are essential. In the climate of the humid tropics, invertebrate animals, including insects, and funguses multiply prolifically where food is available for them. A plantation represents a vast store for those that can find food in it and they can cause appalling devastation.

Yet pesticides cannot be applied in ways that will interfere with neighbouring natural forest. They cannot be sprayed from the air, for example. The pesticides must be supplied, together with the equipment needed to use them safely.

Once established, a tropical plantation can satisfy more needs than the kind of conifer plantation with which we are familiar. Obviously, it produces timber, but timber of uniform and predictable quality with yields up to thirty times those available from an equivalent area of natural forest. It produces small wood, for fencing and making craft products for the use of local people or for export. Depending on the species chosen, it may produce fruits, nuts, fibres, or plants with medicinal values for local use. The plantation can be integrated into local agriculture. Its foliage can be harvested to feed livestock, and the trees themselves can provide shade for animals or for other plant crops.

Shell, for example, has made it an explicit part of its policy not to undertake natural forest clearance nor to conduct any forestry operations which may damage irrevocably the natural forest environment, and it is one of the companies that has been most active in establishing plantations. These now amount to about 230 000 hectares (575 000 acres) in South America, Africa, Asia, and New Zealand.

The countries of the humid tropics include some of the poorest in the world. They must be helped to develop economically, but in ways that allow their own people to participate fully in the sustainable exploitation of local resources. Working in partnership with local people and with their governments, and building on the forestry sciences and techniques that grew out of our response to the deforestation of Europe and the United States, industry is now able to make a major contribution to this development and to the protection of the forests that remain undisturbed.

Tropical rainforest

Tropical forests develop where the average temperature is about 27 °C (81 °F), and rainforests develop where the rainfall is more than about 2000 millimetres (80 inches) per year. It can be much wetter than this. In parts of Cameroon 10 000 millimetres (400 inches) of rain have been recorded in a year. Within the tropics, however, not all forests are correctly described as rainforests. In some places, conditions are too dry and, on mountainsides, they are too cool, and montane forests develop, with a different botanical composition.

Within a tropical rainforest, moisture is abundant and, above the canopy, the sunlight is intense but the soil is often shallow and sometimes waterlogged. The tropical forests are ancient. Their composition has changed with changes in climate but, even during the series of ice ages that ended about 10 000 years ago, much of the present tropical-forest area was forested. This long history has produced very old soils in which plant nutrients are depleted. The forests contain their nutrients in the living plants which are recycled rapidly when a plant dies.

The forest is three-dimensional. Dominated by tall trees, many rising to 30 metres (100 feet) or more, there is an understorey of smaller trees and, beneath them, one or more layers of young trees and shrubs. In a closed-canopy forest, much of the ground is deeply shaded and the rain drips down from leaf to leaf. Except in gaps opened by the death of a large tree that has fallen and brought other smaller trees down with it, there are few non-woody herbs. Instead of herbs, there are epiphytes, plants such as bromeliads, some ferns, mosses, and lichens, that grow on the surface of larger plants but depend on them only for support. They are not parasites. Animals, too, are distributed vertically and some species seldom leave the layer in which they live. This complex structure, evolved over a very long time, gives the tropical rain forest its uniquely rich diversity of species.

PRESERVING THE FOREST

The largest area of tropical rainforest is centred on the Amazon Basin in South America. It covers some 400 million hectares (1000 million acres) and accounts for about one-sixth of the world's broadleaved forest, but about 1 per cent of it is being cleared each year.

The preservation of the richest of the tropical rainforests depends on the success with which enterprises can be developed that allow people to grow food, obtain fuel, and manufacture goods for sale without encroaching on undisturbed forest. Modern industry can make a major contribution to the attainment of this goal.

Aerial view of rainforest canopy in southwest Cameroon.

CHAPTER 5
STONE

We cannot help changing the natural environment around us. Everything we do produces some effect but, in most cases, nature will reverse the changes, given time. If we gave up farming, for example, within a century or two something much like the original forest or grassland would establish itself, and there would be little evidence of our former interventions.

Quarrying is an exception to the rule. When we take away the rock itself, the very stuff from which the land is made, scarring is unavoidable and, unless we take deliberate steps to restore it, the scar will be permanent.

This does not necessarily mean the long-term effect will be harmful. Scars may remain visible, at least to those who know how to recognize them, but they

Quarrying disfigures the landscape, but the quarries can be screened and, when work ceases, modern practice requires the site to be restored. This quarry produces roadstone.

imply no lasting injury to the natural environment. Scars, after all, indicate past damage that has healed. Plants return when the workers depart, and animals arrive to feed on the plants. A freshly

---

A freshly abandoned quarry may look unattractive but it is of great value to those studying the record of our planet's history.

---

abandoned quarry may look unattractive but it is of great value to those studying the record of our planet's history. Much of our geological knowledge has come from the detailed examination of the sections through rock formations that have been cut by quarrymen. Nowadays, a professional geologist must receive a formal education in the subject but it was not always so, and some of the most famous names in the history of the various branches of geology started life as quarrymen or stonemasons. Hugh Miller (1802-56), for example, was apprenticed to a stonemason but, for most of his life, earned his living by writing and as editor of an Edinburgh newspaper called *Witness*. He wrote a series of articles for the paper and, in 1841, republished them as a book, *The Old Red Sandstone*, describing his geological discoveries in his native Cromarty. The book is one of the classics of geological writing. People still read it.

Later, after the geologists have gone and natural colonization has begun, an old quarry acquires a new importance, as an area of habitat, probably undisturbed by humans for it no longer has any commercial value, that is different from the surrounding environment. It becomes a refuge, rich in species that may be uncommon or even rare.

This is true of small quarries, abandoned because the stone was found to be of inferior quality, or demand fell and the company went out of business, or because the supply of good stone was small and eventually exhausted. More successful working quarries are sometimes large and, where they contain stone with special qualities or attractive appearance, they may remain in operation for a long time. The quarry at Carrara, Italy, is still producing the pure, white marble it once supplied to Michelangelo and, at a more mundane level, Croft quarry, in the East Midlands of England, is still producing a pink granite used mainly to build roads 2000 years after the Romans used similar stone from the same quarry to surface the Fosse Way.

THE PLACE VALUE OF STONE

Carrara marble is transported long distances. The transport adds greatly to the cost of a material that is already expensive because it is in great demand, but rich patrons are willing to pay for sculptures carved from it. This is unusual. Cheap modern transport has increased the range within which particular stone can be used but, in general, quarries serve only their immediate locality. Stone is bulky and heavy. It is also very common, and the cost of transporting it more than a short distance raises the price to a level higher than that of stone from quarries nearer at hand. Like any mineral, stone can be quarried only where it is found and therefore it has a 'place value' determined by its location and special qualities. The greater the demand, the more likely it is that customers will be willing to meet the cost of transport. Modern city buildings are often faced with stone quarried far away and used purely for its decorative value.

Such use of expensive stone is deliberately ostentatious, proclaiming the wealth, authority, and reliability of its owner. This is nothing new, nor is the transport of suitable stone over long distances for this

The Sphinx was carved from a single outcrop of rock. The pyramids were built from blocks of different stones, some transported over long distances. Each type of stone had a particular use.

purpose. The mere fact of its transport implies wealth and power and, in ancient times, it provided a clear demonstration of the fact that a society could spare workers for long periods from the tasks, such as growing food, necessary for subsistence. The society had surplus wealth. What could be more awe-inspiring than the Pyramids, more enigmatic than the Sphinx, or more mysterious than Stonehenge?

The Sphinx was carved from a rock outcrop during the ancient Egyptian Fourth Dynasty but pyramids were built from the earliest times, from stone that was often moved many miles. The Great Pyramid of Khufu, said to be the largest building ever constructed, is made from more than 2 million stone blocks, each weighing an average of 2.5 tonnes but with some weighing 16 tonnes — a total of nearly 6 million tonnes of stone — some of granite, others of limestone, each of them chosen for the part of the structure where their particular qualities were

most needed. Stonehenge was built in stages separated by long intervals but, not only has the source of its bluestones been traced to the Preseli Hills, across the Bristol Channel in Pembrokeshire, but the route has been traced by which they were transported.

The Great Pyramid may be the largest building, but the greatest construction project the world has ever seen was the creation of the Great Wall of China. Extending for nearly 2500 kilometres (1550 miles), it was completed in the third century BC by linking existing walls and adding new sections, since when it has been much modified. It was made

... the greatest construction project the world has ever seen ...

from earth and stone, and its eastern section was faced with brick. There is no reason to suppose it was built from other than locally acquired materials but, after all this time, no trace remains of whatever environmental disruption the project may have caused.

A PART OF THE LANDSCAPE

Important monuments may be built from materials moved long distances from their source, but stone houses are invariably built from local materials so that they give an area a particular visual quality that reflects the underlying geology. They seem to sit well in the landscape for the excellent reason that their colours and textures repeat those to be seen in the stones lying around on nearby fields, in gateposts, and on and beside the surface of country lanes. For this reason, **stone is** perhaps the most aesthetically satisfying of all building materials, even if it does have

to be taken from large, ugly, noisy, dusty quarries.

Their long working lives and the highly visible contribution they make to local buildings give quarries another quality that people who have never lived close to one may think unusual. Quarrying is an industry that has continued without interruption throughout the whole of history, and quarries are accepted in their own neighbourhoods. Far from objecting to their presence, most local people either ignore them, or are proud of them and often very knowledgeable about the characteristics of the stone they contain. The quarries provide employment for generation after generation of families whose accumulated experience builds into a familiarity with the material they work equal to that which a skilled woodcarver has with wood, a forester with trees, or a farmer with his land.

The building of the Great Wall of China, seen here north of Beijing, was the world's greatest construction project.

... the most aesthetically satisfying of all building materials, ...

Stone blocks provide walls, but roofs are more commonly made from tiles, a ceramic product, or from slate. Slate is quarried like any other stone but, although slate is a common type of metamorphosed sedimentary rock, deposits of a quality high enough to make them commercially valuable occur in only a limited number of places. To be useful the slate must split easily into flat sections and be hard and impermeable enough to afford complete protection against water. In addition to roofs, slates are also used to clad the outside of buildings — 'hung slate' houses are attractive, well protected, and typical of certain areas — and find uses wherever it is necessary to produce a completely flat, solid surface. Slate covered with green baize is what makes snooker and pool tables so smooth, so solid, and so heavy. Slate is sometimes an attractive rock and, in the regions that produce it, small local firms earn a useful additional income from the sale of slate ornaments and carvings.

Where they do occur, commercial slate deposits are often extensive and the quarries large. Blaenau Ffestiniog, in Wales, is a town dominated by its dark slate, and at Delabole, in North Cornwall, the slate quarry occupies what local people claim is the largest hole in Britain. Again, the effect on the environment appears to be devastating and far beyond any possibility of reclamation, for the 'Delabole hole' is far too wide and deep ever to be filled and the Blaenau quarries and their waste tips cover a vast area, yet the slate workings are accepted calmly. They are even exploited as tourist attractions.

The use of local building materials, seen here at Broadway, in Hereford and Worcester, produces a unifying theme of colours and textures that is visually attractive.

THE PRICE OF ROCK

The fortunes of large quarries are linked intimately with prices and with the technology available for working them. Remove rock from a hole and the hole will become steadily deeper. This increases the height through which the rock has to be lifted as it is removed, and lifting heavy objects is difficult and expensive. Eventually a point may be reached where the cost of removing the rock makes it more expensive than rock from shallower quarries. Sales fall, the operation becomes uneconomic, and the quarry may have to close. Then a new way is found to move rock more cheaply and the quarry can resume work. A century ago, rock was often hauled out of a quarry in railway wagons pulled by horses. Then the operation was mechanized and the wagons were winched up from the face. More recently still, the rails have gone and the trucks have rubber wheels. Where the material to be carried is small, conveyor belts are used.

The method of extracting rock has also changed. Explosives are still used to blast away sections of the face, but they can be used much more precisely because lasers are employed to measure the face accurately. The measurements allow the best place to locate the charges to be calculated accurately and there is less waste of explosive and of rock. It is cheaper and also safer, and the older explosives, such as dynamite, are being replaced by substances that are safer to store and use.

The expansion of the railway network in the last century brought much work for quarries for, although the railway may have been made from iron, the iron rails had to be laid on a prepared base. The base had to be level, sufficiently flexible to absorb the weight of a passing train, and had to drain well. The material chosen to build it was hard rock that had been crushed to produce small stones all of more or less the same size.

Slate is common, but slate suitable for roofing is not and, where it occurs, the quarries are usually large, as here at Llanberis, North Wales. Plants soon colonize ledges where work has ceased.

The rail network was barely completed before road transport became popular; road vehicles acquired rubber tyres that were rapidly destroyed by surfaces adequate for the iron-clad wheels of horse-drawn wagons and carriages, and more crushed stone and gravel was needed for the building of modern, smooth-surfaced roads. When you drive along a major modern road, you see only its surface but the road is much more than just a layer of asphalt or concrete. It has several layers and the quarries contribute to them all.

Below the road there lies the 'subgrade', the natural rock or subsoil on which the road is built. Above the subgrade is the 'sub-base', a layer of irregularly shaped stones that pack together in such a way as to leave air spaces between them. The sub-base provides support and the spaces between the stones allow water to drain

Above left: *Railways use large quantities of stone to make a surface on which to set the rails. This railway is in Mauritania, West Africa.*
Above: *Several layers of stone lie below the surface of this road, in the Mojave Desert, California.*

and permit water to expand and contract as it freezes and thaws without causing the road to subside or rise. A further layer of stones, the 'road base', is laid on top of the sub-base to provide the main support for the road. The stones of the road base may be loose or cemented together. Above the road base there is the 'basecourse'. This is made from crushed rock or gravel. It provides drainage and distributes the weight of the road evenly on to the road base. Finally there is the 'wearing course', which is the part of the road that you see. It has to be impermeable, durable, and as traffic moves over it, gradually wearing it down, the surface must not become polished.

The Croft quarry, now owned by English China Clays, produces a stone that is highly resistant to polishing and that tends to form regular cubes when it is crushed. Croft is one of many quarries supplying stone mainly for road construction, and it is big. Annual production approaches 3 million tonnes. The working area occupies 100 hectares (250 acres) and the stone is removed in 'benches', steps 12 metres (almost 40 feet) high with a narrow ledge at the foot of each. There are now ten benches, and the quarry is 120 metres (almost 400 feet) deep. The

rock, a distinctive pink granite, is removed by blasting, then crushed in huge machines — controlled by computer, of course — to 30-centimetre (12-inch) cubes, which are then crushed further and screened to make sure they are of a standard size. Although the quarry was worked in Roman times, its modern revival began in 1868 when it supplied stone ballast for the railway line being laid very close by, between Birmingham and Leicester. Then it benefited from being the nearest source of hard rock during the expansion of London and the towns of south-east England.

SYNTHETIC STONE

Although we may think of quarried stone mainly as a material cut in solid blocks and used for building, stone is no longer the most common construction material, and solid blocks are no longer the most important product of quarries. The change came as the result of a long search for a material that would bind stones together and resist water. The pyramids were built using a mortar made from gypsum (calcium sulphate), the Greeks used slaked lime (calcium hydroxide), and the Romans found that mortar could be made waterproof if a certain volcanic rock, found near the town of Pozzuoli, or powdered fragments of pottery, were mixed with it. For centuries, this remained the only way known to make a waterproof mortar but when, in 1756, John Smeaton planned to build the Eddystone lighthouse off Plymouth, he improved on the recipe by adding a large amount of clay to the limestone. Smeaton's original lighthouse was replaced, and his tower moved to Plymouth Hoe where it is now a tourist attraction. Others continued to experiment and, in

1824, John Aspdin took out a patent on a material he called 'Portland cement' because it looked to him like the excellent and very popular limestone used in many buildings and quarried at Portland, in Dorset.

Portland cement was not only a satisfactory mortar. It could be used as a structural material in its own right and, in the years since, stone blasted from quarries as a construction material has given way to a synthetic stone made in factories from mined and quarried raw materials. Modern Portland cement is made from a rock containing limestone and clay mixed with

Cement is one of the most useful of all building materials and it is an industrial product, invented about 150 years ago. This is the Blue Circle cement works at Westbury, Wiltshire.

Modern quarries ... have to take account of the environmental consequences ...

a variety of ingredients that can include limestone, chalk or sea shells, clay, sand, and a source of iron, depending on what is available to produce the correct proportions of lime, silica (sand), alumina (clay), and iron. When the basic ingredients have been processed, gypsum is added.

The processing involves crushing then grinding the rock, blending the resulting powder to produce the correct mixture, which is heated in a kiln to about 1500 °C (2700 °F) to convert the limestone (calcium carbonate) into lime (calcium oxide) by driving off carbon dioxide, and finally by grinding the clinker produced in the kiln and adding gypsum. When the finished powder is mixed with water, a complex series of chemical reactions occurs that bind the cement together into a solid mass. Cement manufacture is an industrial operation carried out on a large scale, but it produces a standardized material whose properties can be modified as required for particular uses.

QUARRIES AND THE ENVIRONMENT

When stone is crushed, the production of dust is unavoidable and, at one time, this dust was tolerated. Workers inhaled it and it damaged their health, and the surrounding countryside was coated with it. Today, the dangers of inhaling stone dust are well known, and so is the way to prevent its release. Where the dust is generated, a fine mist of water is sprayed into the air to coat the particles and make them settle. It is no more than an industrial-scale version of the time-honoured technique of scattering water on to a dusty floor to make it easier to sweep. Sometimes anti-pollution strategies are

Our buildings say a great deal about our view of ourselves. Far left: The Guggenheim Museum in New York was designed by Frank Lloyd Wright. Above: The 'lost city' of Macchu Picchu, in the Cuzco region of Peru, discovered in 1911.

technically complicated. In this case, the remedy is simplicity itself and it is highly effective.

Modern quarries, like other industrial installations, have to take account of the environmental consequences of their activities, and their owners must behave responsibly. In most countries this is the law but it is also good mining practice. When a deposit of commercially exploitable rock is identified, a mining company cannot merely move in with its machinery and start working, as it might have done a century ago. The operation begins with a detailed study of the site and its surroundings to provide the information that is used to produce a plan of the entire operation, from the time the first worker arrives until the deposit is exhausted and the site restored. Drawings are made — artists' impressions of what the place will look like at each stage — and models may be built. These are used in discussions with the planning authorities and local residents.

Many things are possible if they can be agreed long in advance and incorporated into the planning. It is possible, for example, to agree with the local community the purpose for which the land will

Limestone pavement is threatened because of the ease with which the stones can be removed. This example, with an ash tree, is near Malham, in the Yorkshire Dales.

ing vegetation, the only limits to what is possible are those imposed by the climate.

The working quarry will be hidden so far as possible so it causes the minimum of visual intrusion. This means locating buildings in the least conspicuous places. Trees will be planted to screen the site and, if trees alone are not enough, earth banks, called 'bunds', may surround the site and be planted with grasses and other herbs, or with trees. English China Clays, for example, has its own tree nursery to supply trees for the purpose, and the trees in the nursery are grown from seeds gathered locally. School children have sometimes been recruited to help in this task as part of their school project work, for it familiarizes them with the tree species found in their neighbourhood and with the composition of local woodlands. The use of locally acquired seed guarantees that the trees the company plants will thrive and that they will blend harmoniously into the countryside.

Access to the quarry must be adequate for the use of the huge vehicles that will be needed, but these vehicles must not be allowed to interfere unduly with other road users. It is unacceptable to have fleets of large trucks passing frequently through village streets or along narrow country lanes. The company may have to build roads of its own and, once it accepts the need for a system of private roads, it can route them in such a way as to keep them largely separate from public roads. It may even be possible to keep them out of sight.

Cement is sometimes used by itself but, more commonly, the powder is mixed with sand, gravel, or both to make concrete, a stronger material than cement, and cheaper because sand and gravel are cheap. As the use of concrete has increased, so has the demand for sand and gravel. These are not massively solid,

be used when quarrying ceases. People may wish it to be restored to the use it had before quarrying began, and this is often possible. It may be, however, that the amenity or even economic value of the site can be enhanced. If it starts as derelict land, left behind when an older industry departed long ago, people might welcome its improvement, perhaps to parkland, or woodland, or even a nature reserve. It need not all be dry land. Ponds and lakes can be included if that is what the community would prefer. So far as a large, modern company is concerned, it makes little difference. Because a company has no intention of leaving the land as a raw, worked-out quarry site, the earth-moving machines that will rebuild it can as easily make ponds, lakes, or hills as level ground and, when it comes to establish-

Sedimentary rocks may contain fossils of great scientific interest — provided they remain in place. The oyster shells in this Argentinian formation are twenty million years old.

although a geologist would describe them as types of rock. They are gathered by stripping away the surface cover and then scooping them out of what become pits.

THE VALUE OF ROCKS

Particular rock formations may be of great scientific value. They can be protected from industrial exploitation but it is much more difficult to defend them against small-scale, and nowadays usually illegal, depradations. In some places, for example, limestone forms more or less horizontal beds, broken by crevices, that becomes exposed through the weathering away of overlying material. This is 'limestone pavement' and it is always botanically important because of the often rare plants that grow in the crevices. Limestone pavements occur in many parts of the world, and they are endangered wherever they are easily accessible because the limestone can be broken into convenient and attractive blocks for use as garden ornaments. The blocks are highly prized, so they have a low place value, and can be sold profitably far from their source. There are now blocks of British limestone decorating Japanese gardens.

Fossils, too, are very popular and, in most cases, are small enough to be used as household ornaments. The study of fossils is crucial to our unravelling of the history of the Earth but, to be of scientific use, the fossils must be examined wherever they occur naturally, for their precise position is used to interpret the material above and below them. Once removed, they are of little use and the value of the formation from which they were taken is much reduced.

Geologists now have a code of practice that, among other things, forbids the removal of rock and fossils from the more important sites. At one time, geologists

could be recognized by the hammers they carried, but hammers are now much less common and they are banned on many excursions. Commercial 'poachers' have invaded many fossil-rich sites, however, and remove large quantities which they sell all over the world.

THE CONCRETE AND THE CLAY

The use of stone blocks for building has declined as other materials have proved cheaper, but those newer materials are obtained by quarrying or mining. Concrete is a synthetic stone, but made from rock that has been broken down and reassembled. Brick, a ceramic product, is made from clay, which is dug from the ground. Timber is the only non-mineral building material and even that may be used only to provide a framework that is filled with brick, stone, or, as 'daub and wattle', smaller wood faced with mud, and mud is dug from the ground. Perhaps one day a new substance will be invented that is better and cheaper than rock, but it seems unlikely.

Old quarries recover when their working lives come to an end. Modern quarries are planned in such a way as to minimize the environmental harm they do during their working lives and to rehabilitate the site when eventually they close, and quarry companies do not damage sites of scientific value. The principal danger to those sites arises from the high prices paid for ornaments and the greed of those who supply them.

REVITALIZING DISUSED GRAVEL PITS

When work ends at a sand or gravel pit, it leaves behind a large, often deep depression. Left to itself, the pit may fill with water and it has been estimated that, in Britain, this is the fate of nine pits out of ten. Because sand and gravel have a high place value, pits are as close as they can be to the urban areas where the sand and gravel are used, and it was not long before people discovered the many attractions of these artificial lakes.

This has led the Sand and Gravel Association to devise and sponsor schemes to enhance the value of worked-out pits. Many are restored as public amenities, to be used for water sports, angling, or other leisure pursuits. Where the pits are far from the sea or from any large natural lake, local people are given access to such activities for the first time, with the added benefit that learning to water-ski or to windsurf on an artificial lake is very much safer than doing so on the sea or in a tidal estuary.

Others become wildlife sanctuaries. The water attracts aquatic birds and the banks are eventually colonized by plants, but the habitat value can be increased, and some

companies now plan for this kind of final use before mineral extraction begins. The Ryton Gravel Company, in north-eastern England, started restoring its pits the moment each stage of extraction ended, so accelerating the colonization by plants, and colonization was helped by the planting of appropriate species. The boundaries of each pit were made irregular and designed to have promontories and bays to increase the length of shoreline when the lake formed. Islands were

made to provide protected nesting sites, and sufficient shallow areas were provided to allow mud to collect and wading birds to feed. Finally, the company installed hides for birdwatchers and other facilities for visitors. The result was a nature reserve in which more than 120 species of birds have been recorded.

This is one of a number of disused pits that are now nature reserves, and many gravel companies plan their pit restoration in collaboration with conservation bodies.

This represents a particularly important contribution to wildlife conservation. Most natural wetlands now receive some protection but many have been lost over the last fifty years by being drained and converted to farm or building land. The creation of new wetland habitat replaces some of what has been lost and conservationists welcome it warmly.

This abandoned chalk quarry in Surrey has been colonized by plants including buddleia, silver birch, and hawthorn that, in turn, will attract insects and other small animals.

CHAPTER 6
FUEL

Visit any of the isolated homes or villages that lie on the plains of northern Europe and Asia, where few trees grow and the climate is cool and wet, and, as you watch the blue smoke curling from the chimneys, you may detect the distinctive aroma of burning peat. Wood was the first fuel to be used, but it cannot have been long after humans first settled in these bleak northern climes that peat was discovered.

PEAT CUTTING AND THE LANDSCAPE

Over the long centuries since, the communities that rely on peat have learned much about its properties and have developed special tools for cutting it. In spring or early summer, the peat is cut in blocks, about the size and shape of house bricks, from vertical faces on the sides of trenches. It is back-breaking work but, in a few days, the men of a family can cut enough fuel to last the household through the winter. The peat blocks are left beside the trench to begin drying, then collected and taken home where they are built into walls outside the house. The fuel dries during the rest of the year so it is ready for use when the cold weather comes, being taken from the wall, still in its blocks, as it is needed.

Peat forms slowly as, year after year, dead plants accumulate in acid, waterlogged ground where the organisms responsible for decomposition cannot survive. This is in Skye.

Not all peat is suitable for use as fuel. Where it is, its quality varies widely, even in a single trench, and the peat-cutters can recognize at a glance the blocks that will be used to light a fire, those that will burn with the most heat, and those that will be used to damp down a fire so it burns slowly through the night. This variation is to be expected because of the way peat forms. It occurs in bogs, where the ground is waterlogged for most of the time and very acid. When vegetation dies only the topmost layer, exposed to the air, decomposes fully. The remainder becomes sodden and, as the years pass and more surface plants die, it is packed together by the weight of overlying material, air is excluded, and decomposition is only partial. When a peat block is teased apart, it is possible to identify many of the plants that compose it.

Peat is the traditional fuel in places where people had no more convenient alternative. It is still dug as it always has been in parts of Ireland, the Scottish islands, and other places in northern Europe. These days, however, it is also cut on an industrial scale, for example in Ireland, the USSR, Germany, and Scandinavia, to be burned in power stations.

When peat is cut and removed, little by little, the landscape is altered, and it is peat cutting that produced one of England's oldest industrial landscapes. In Norfolk and Suffolk, the area that is now the Broads was once reed swamp, marsh, dry land, and peat bog, formed after the end of the last glaciation. As the great depth of peat was cut, little by little, the trenches widened and filled with water. The cutting was especially intensive in medieval times, when it is estimated that some 25 million cubic metres (880 million cubic feet) of peat were removed. Then, in the fourteenth century, the sea invaded to convert the trenches into a pattern of fifty shallow lakes linked by nearly 200 kilometres (125 miles) of rivers, interspersed low-lying, rolling

Top: *Traditional peat cutting, seen here on the Isle of Jura in the Hebrides, involves cutting brick-shaped blocks of peat from trenches. These men will collect enough peat to supply their homes with fuel through the coming year.* Above: *Machines which can remove peat quickly and in large amounts change the landscape rapidly and may destroy communities of unusual plants. This scene is in the Flow Country of Caithness.*

countryside, woodland, and marshes. It is attractive now, but 500 years ago it would have looked ravaged. Landscapes usually recover, given enough time.

Modern, mechanized peat-cutting, however, changes landscapes at unprecedented speed, and peat bogs are now recognized as having great botanical importance. These wet, acid, inhospitable places support communities of plants that

Coal mining transforms landscapes but, when the mines close, the buildings can be removed, spoil heaps landscaped, and the site restored. This mine is in Wales.

are adapted to the conditions and that survive nowhere else. The cutting of peat threatens to destroy many areas of valuable habitat, and the draining of bogs to reclaim the land for forestry or agriculture threatens still more. In the far north-east of Scotland, plans to establish plantation forest over a large part of the Flow Country, the largest area of blanket bog in Britain, were modified following a storm of protest from conservationists, but it was not long before the peat was being mined for export as power-station fuel.

COAL — A TRUE FOSSIL FUEL

A product of arrested decomposition, peat is classed as one of the 'fossil' fuels, fuels that are taken from the ground, as are minerals, but that are of organic rather than mineral origin. The vegetation that produced peat is no more than centuries, or a few thousands of years old. Coal is usually 300 to 400 million years old — a true fossil material in which real fossils are often found and, these days, preserved for

scientific study. Its formation began in much the same way as peat, although in tropical environments, but it was then hardened by being compressed beneath a great weight of sediment, and buried, often deep below ground. The processes to which it was subjected were similar to those that alter a muddy sediment into a sedimentary rock. The coal occurs in seams, seldom more than a few metres thick, and, as mining operations follow the seams, mines can become very deep. In the underground mines of Britain the average working depth is now about 350 metres (1150 feet) and the average seam thickness is 1.6 metres (5^1/$_4$ feet).

The value of a combustible fuel depends on the proportion of carbon it contains as compared to the proportions of moisture and 'volatiles' — substances that vaporize and are lost as the fuel is warmed. Using this measure, fuels can be arranged in order of rank, starting with wood which is the least efficient, then proceeding through peat, lignite, sub-bituminous and bituminous coals, to anthracite which is the most efficient of all.

Lignite is either brown or black and often rather crumbly in texture. Although it occurs widely and accounts for about half of all the coal in the world, it is little used except close to the deposits. It deteriorates if it is stored in the open, and its inferiority, compared with other coals, means it is uneconomic to transport it over long distances. Like peat, however, it is found at or very close to the surface, making it relatively easy and cheap to obtain. The higher ranking, sub-bituminous and bituminous coals are won either by mining below ground or, where the seams lie close to the surface, by opencast mining.

The burning of coal in open grates produces smoke and a range of gaseous and particulate pollutants, but the extent of the pollution is linked closely to the

When organic matter is processed to make it burn at a higher temperature, the result is charcoal, still an important fuel in many parts of the world. This charcoal is in Trinidad.

rank of the coal. The smaller the proportion of moisture and volatiles the coal contains, the less pollution its burning causes. Anthracite is the cleanest of all coals. It is said that Queen Victoria insisted that her royal yacht used only anthracite from Pembrokeshire. The dangers attending such pollution were recognized long ago and the first attempts to deal with them were made in England in 1273, when a smoke abatement law was passed, and in 1306, when the burning of coal in London was forbidden by royal decree. The fuel was known as 'sea coal', not because it was mined beneath the sea but because it was transported to London by sea from the north-east of England.

CHARCOAL — FUEL AND FILTER

Most solid fuels can be processed to make them burn at a higher temperature, or more cleanly, or both. For centuries charcoal was the main fuel for iron smelting. It is made by heating wood, or other vegetable matter, in the absence of air,

traditionally by building a large stack of material, partly covering it with earth, igniting it, and allowing it to heat for several days. The process wasted all the by-products and up to three-quarters of the energy value of the raw material. Today it is made much more efficiently, and cleanly, in steel retorts. It is a factory product, and the process is sometimes fuelled by its own output of tar and gas. Charcoal is still an important fuel in many of the less developed countries, and, although it is burned in the industrialized countries mainly in barbecue stoves — a not insignificant market — it has found other uses. It is porous, giving it a very large surface area in relation to its volume, and oxygen, together with any substance dispersed in the oxygen, is readily held on the surface of its pores. This property can be enhanced by heating the charcoal in a restricted flow of air or by adding catalysts during charcoal production to make 'activated charcoal' which is used in water purification, to remove unwanted colours from liquids, and to remove air pollutants. It is very effective at purifying air, and, in World War 1, large amounts were used in gas masks.

'SMOKELESS' COAL AND GAS FROM COAL AND OIL

As coal displaced wood as the main fuel in large cities, a need arose for a fuel which had a combustion temperature high enough to smelt iron and that would be more easily obtainable than charcoal, for in an open grate, coal burns at a fairly low temperature. This need, combined with the desire to reduce smoke emissions and to save coal tar (a useful substance in its own right that is wasted when sub-bituminous coal is burned) led to the invention of the first smokeless fuel. John Evelyn, the diarist, records seeing sea coal being charred, 'to burn out the sulphur and render it sweet', in 1656, and mentions that 'The coal thus charred is sold as *coke*, a very useful fuel'.

Coke is produced by heating coal to about 1100 °C (2000 °F) in the absence of air. This releases the volatiles and leaves behind rather more than half of the original weight of coal as the familiar light, porous, clean fuel which is almost pure carbon. Most coking plants operate to produce fuel for smelting with tar and gas as by-products.

Coal gas consists mainly of carbon monoxide which burns readily with a hot flame. By 1820, companies had been formed to supply it for industrial and

... *at the turn of a knob and the strike of a match,* ...

domestic use in most of the major cities of Europe and North America, and it became one of the most important fuels. It provided street and domestic lighting that was far brighter than any form of lighting known previously. Gas fires were invented to provide space heating, gas stoves to cook food at predictable temperatures that could be controlled at the turn of a knob and the strike of a match, and it was used to power a range of domestic appliances. Eventually gas gave way to electric power for lighting and the operation of most appliances, but it still remains popular for cooking and for space and water heating, although the gas we use today is natural gas and not coal gas. Natural gas, with its main constituent of methane, is a product of the oil industry.

THE GREENHOUSE EFFECT

The burning of any fuel that contains carbon — and the list includes wood, peat, coal, gas, and oil — produces carbon

Charcoal is now made by an industrial process that is cleaner and less wasteful than the traditional method. It burns at a temperature high enough for most industrial purposes. This factory in Thailand is powered by charcoal.

dioxide. This is inevitable because the chemical reaction that releases heat is the rapid oxidation of carbon. Dispersed in the atmosphere, carbon dioxide absorbs long-wave radiation and so contributes to the 'greenhouse effect' that many climatologists believe will radically alter climates over the next century. Other potentially polluting emissions from the combustion of carbon-based fuels can be isolated, so they cannot enter the outside environment, but the emission of carbon dioxide is unavoidable. The only way we can reduce carbon dioxide emissions is to reduce the quantity of carbon-based fuel that we burn.

An age-old fuel

Coal has been mined for a very long time. Aristotle referred to smiths who used a 'black stone' rather than wood, and the Romans used coal, certainly in England and probably elsewhere in Europe. Reporting on his travels in Asia in the late

... throughout the province of Cathay there is a sort of black stone, which ... burns like logs.

thirteenth century, Marco Polo wrote that '... throughout the province of Cathay there is a sort of black stone, which is dug out of veins in the hillsides and burns like logs. ... They do not give off flames, except a little when they are first kindled, just as charcoal does, and once they have caught fire they give out a great heat'. According to his account, the supply of wood was adequate for most purposes but not for the heating of bath water in a region where everyone bathed at least three times a week and where the more prosperous citizens had bathrooms in their houses. Large-scale mining began in

Europe in the fifteenth century, and coal was being mined commercially in the United States by the middle of the eighteenth century.

Encouraging regeneration

When coal is mined, the production of waste is unavoidable and, during the years when coal was the principal fuel driving industrialization, the waste was piled in tips close to the mines. The villages in the coalfields became surrounded by tips. Today many of the older pits have closed, their tips have disappeared, and the landscape is being restored. The mining valleys of South Wales, once blackened, are now evolving into rural areas.

Restoration often involves large earth-moving machinery and the creation of a new topography, but not always. Left undisturbed, tips are colonized by wild plants and eventually a black wasteland may turn green, with a riot of flowers in spring and summer, so what were artificial hills and valleys of mine waste form a new landscape, attractive in itself. The coal industry works in close collaboration with

In time, spoil heaps from coal mines are colonized by plants and, like the one here, become rich in wildlife.

This mine tip, at Pye Hill Colliery in Nottinghamshire, is being restored progressively. Cattle graze the sections that have been reclaimed and, eventually, the entire area will be pasture land.

conservationists and adapts its reclamation techniques to local circumstances.

Bold Moss, for example, is a coal tip, fifty years old and covering 55 hectares (136 acres), from the Bold colliery, not far from the centre of St Helens, Lancashire. The colliery is now closed and, in 1987, British Coal appointed the Groundwork Trust, which specializes in the reclamation of derelict land, to devise a scheme for the tip. The Trust emphasized the natural regeneration already taking place and proposed that encouraging this process would be preferable to engineering a new landscape. It suggested that local people, especially children and the retired, be involved in the project from the start. British Coal responded by selling the land to the Trust for a nominal sum and offering to pay for transforming the area into a country park with woodland that could form part of a proposed Merseyside community forest. The scheme won the backing of the Country-

side Commission which agreed to award it a grant as soon as it received formal approval from the Department of the Environment. Local people will contribute to its planning, and the work, designed to begin in 1990, will provide employment for local young people some of whom might go on to careers in landscape management.

The restoration of waste tips often necessitates measures to reduce the acidity of the soil that is to be planted. The simplest way to achieve this quickly is to add lime, either as calcium hydroxide (slaked lime) or as pulverized limestone. Lime is also used in the scrubbers that remove sulphur from the flue gases in coal-burning plants and so the coal industry has considerable interest in it. One by-product of this interest has been the development of an industrial method

Oil drilling is not necessarily disruptive. This is Furzey Island, Dorset, the site of BP's Wytch Farm oilfield, where one drilling rig is in operation and a second under construction.

for converting limestone into pellets.

Usually, lime is produced as a fine powder and this is the form in which it is used by farmers and gardeners. The powder is satisfactory for most uses, and the finer the powder the more quickly it exerts its chemical effect, but it is difficult to distribute powder from the air when large areas are to be treated because it drifts in the wind. Pellets are less liable to drift and, when they land, they are less prone to being washed away by rain. They break down slowly, which means they continue to deliver their lime over a long period. Pelleted lime has been used in tests over land, and the first five-year stage of a project at Loch Fleet, Scotland, has shown that it improves conditions in acid lakes so that, within a short time, fish can thrive in them.

OPENCAST MINING

Introduced in Britain in 1942 as a war-time emergency measure, opencast workings now produce a large proportion of all the British coal mined. The technique is used throughout the world, wherever coal lies close to the surface. Opencast pits allow access to seams that are too thin or too close to the surface to be worked in any other way, and the coal is often of high quality. Half of the anthracite mined in Britain comes from opencast pits, and pillars of high-rank coal, left behind in some older underground pits to provide roof support, can now be recovered by stripping away the overlying material, the 'overburden'. The overburden is removed in such a way as to separate the coal completely — gentle brushing is sometimes used to clear the final layer — so it can be used without washing, unlike coal from an underground mine. This avoids any need for cleaning washing water to prevent pollution.

Opencast mines are usually large. Many cover 200 to 300 hectares (500 to 750 acres) of land and, although some are small, others are much bigger even than this. The Dalquhandy site in Lanarkshire occupies 1046 hectares (2615 acres) and, at Chalmerston, Ayrshire, the pit is 742 hectares (1855 acres) in area. The pits are short-lived, however. Most are exhausted in ten years or less, and even the large ones, remain open for less than twenty years. Work began in 1988 at both Chalmerston and Dalquhandy and will finish at Chalmerston in 1997 and at Dalquhandy in 2005.

The environmental cost of such large operations is obvious. An average of 30 tonnes of overburden must be removed for every tonne of coal recovered, and the eventual pit may be more, sometimes much more, than 80 metres (260 feet) deep. The devastation is on a vast scale and, because of this, the planning of an opencast pit includes the restoration of the site when work is finished. Every year in Britain several former sites are returned to other uses. Many have been restored for agricultural use but now the European Community tends to over-produce food the emphasis has changed and sites are being prepared for amenity uses or wild-life conservation.

Opencast sites do not always begin as green fields. Coal seams usually occur in industrial areas, for obvious reasons, and so pits may be opened on what, in fact, is derelict land. This affords new opportunities. The damage of earlier times can be repaired and the land returned to the community in a much improved condition.

THE OIL INDUSTRY

Petroleum, also a fossil fuel, has been used since ancient times, mainly for its non-fuel products although it was burned in lamps. Bitumen was used in Mesopotamia and Persia, in mortar and as an adhesive for such things as mosaics and precious stones. Marco Polo found it being extracted commercially in Persia. The modern oil industry, however, did not begin until the middle of the last century. The first successful oil well is usually said to be the one opened by Edwin Drake in Titusville, Pennsylvania, in 1859.

A mobile jack-up rig, used to drill at a slant, moving into position in the British Gas Morecambe gas field. Another drilling platform and the central offshore complex are in the background.

Oil and gas pipelines

Oil, in its various forms, and natural gas are transported by sea, rail, and road, but most commonly of all by pipeline. When natural gas replaced coal gas in Britain, a gas pipe was laid right across East Anglia to bring in the supply from the North Sea, and, in Scotland, a pipeline more than 220 kilometres (137 miles) long runs from St Fergus, on the coast north of Aberdeen, to Mossmorran and on to Braefoot Bay, in Fife, carrying a number of liquid fuels intermediate between crude oil and gas.

The word 'pipeline' suggests a single length of piping, but a pipeline often consists of several large pipes laid in parallel. The Scottish pipeline comprises six separate pipes.

In the Middle East, where pipelines cross sparsely inhabited desert, the pipes are laid on the surface for economy and ease of maintenance. They cross Alaska mounted a little above the surface to avoid disturbing the permanently frozen ground. In more densely populated, temperate countries, such as those of Europe, an overland pipeline passes across farm land and forests, under roads and rivers — the Scottish pipeline crosses the rivers Dee and Tay — and around towns, villages, and important historical sites. It must be buried.

The prospective route is surveyed and photographed to make sure that, when work is completed, the land is restored precisely to its former state. Communities who will be affected by the work are consulted and kept fully informed, for their co-operation is vital.

Installing the oil pipe from Cruden Bay, Aberdeenshire, to Grangemouth Refinery. Below left: Trenching through farm land in Perthshire. Below: The trench being filled. Right: The same scene as it is now. There is no visible trace of the large BP oil pipeline that crosses this peaceful countryside. Routine monitoring from the air makes sure no sign of it appears.

The topsoil is removed from one section at a time, and stored. Techniques developed during the installation of the North Sea gas pipeline through East Anglia make it possible for mature trees to be removed, their roots, still with the soil attached, sealed in plastic, and stored safely until it is time for them to be replaced. They survive the treatment and ensure that the trees along the route are not merely similar to those that grew there before but are literally the same trees.

No sign of disturbance

As the pipes are laid, the trench is filled, the topsoil returned, and the contours restored so the line of the route cannot be seen as a linear bulge or depression. The soil is cultivated, the original trees and shrubs are returned, and other plants are sown.

After a few years, only the most expert eye can detect any sign of the disturbance. The route is monitored by helicopter at regular intervals to make sure the pipeline remains undetectable and, should any sign of it appear, remedial action is taken.

Left: *So far as seabirds are concerned, the oil jetties at Teesmouth provide convenient places to rest between fishing trips.*
Right: *If gases escaping under pressure from oil wells were not ignited, they might accumulate and cause accidents. The flames of the Middle Eastern oil fields are visible from space. This oil well is in Saudi Arabia.*

Oil is formed from the remains of marine organisms that fell to the sea bed, partially decomposed, were carried into places where they accumulated and became sealed beneath overlying rocks, and were then heated. The resulting amorphous material is often mixed with very salt water. Subsequent crustal movements may bring oil deposits close enough to the surface for oil to seep out above the ground and it can be also be extracted from certain shales — soft sedimentary rocks — but most oil is obtained by drilling through the overlying rock and so tapping the reservoir.

It is important that as much oil as possible is extracted from a reservoir. When the cap over the reservoir is first pierced the pressure under which the oil and gas are held is sufficient to make them flow, but as the pressure is relieved the flow slackens and eventually ceases — but with as much as two-thirds of the oil still held in the reservoir.

Winning this remaining oil, by a process called 'secondary recovery', involves pumping a fluid into the well down one hole until it flows up again through another. The chemical industry assists in this operation by inventing and manufacturing substances that soften oil that has hardened and ease oil away from the rock pores in which it is trapped. Such substances must remain stable at the high temperatures they are likely to encounter as they are pressurized, they must not be affected by contact with the brine associated with the oil, and they must not become so viscous they cease to pour readily. Oil companies have been very active in developing such products.

The extraction of oil, from wells rather than from mines, causes less disturbance to the landscape than does coal mining, but the equipment employed in drilling is large and noisy. Where it takes place close to dwellings, local people must be consulted at every stage.

Estuarine operations necessitate even more careful planning. Estuaries are used by many people, for commercial fishing, transport, and increasingly for recreation, and they are of great importance ecologically. Before work can begin, detailed studies are made of the bed of the estuary and of tides and water currents that determine the way sediment moves and is deposited. A large structure fixed to the bed in the wrong place could alter sedi-

Offshore installations must also respect marine life.

mentary processes in ways that damaged salt marshes and mudflats, which are feeding grounds for many birds. Wrecks must be located and interference with them avoided, for they may be graves or of archaeological interest.

Offshore installations must also respect marine life. Because of their isolation, the industrial and domestic wastes they produce are processed on the platform. The reservoir water that is mixed with the oil is passed through separators to remove any remaining oil and then discharged

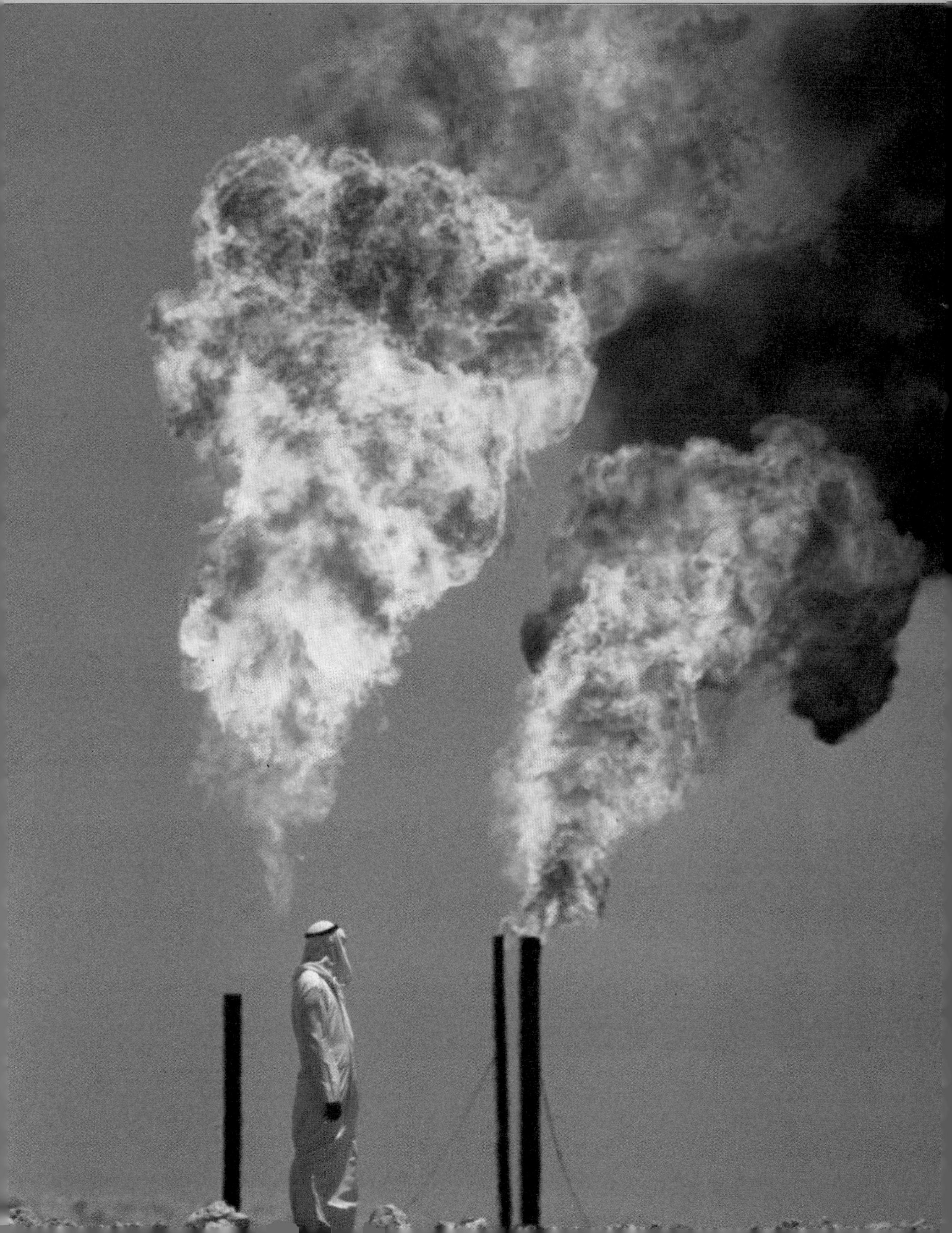

into the sea beneath the platform. Biodegradable domestic wastes are also discharged into the sea after they have been ground into small fragments. Solid wastes are compacted and returned to shore. The whole process is monitored constantly using mussels, kept in cages and examined from time to time to discover whether they have concentrated pollutants in their bodies. Fears that oil platforms might be injurious to seabirds have proved unfounded. Migrating birds often rest on them but otherwise birds seem to ignore them — although there are conflicting views about the effects on migrating birds of gas flares in the North Sea.

Oil cannot be used in the form in which it is extracted. It has to be refined, and oil refineries are big and, to most people, ugly. Eventually they, too, reach the end of their useful lives and must be decommissioned. At Oakville, Ontario, a Shell Canada refinery processing 44 000 barrels of oil a day — about 8 million litres (1.75

Above: *While it awaits refining, crude oil must be stored. This BP storage installation is at Dalmeny, Scotland. The site is not attractive, but eventually it can be restored.* Right: *The sun sets over oil rigs in the North Sea.*

million gallons) — was closed in 1983 because of the falling demand for petroleum. Its site, covering 222 hectares (555 acres), became the first ever to be returned to commercial and residential use. An operation that took six years and cost an estimated Can $4 million began when all hydrocarbons were removed and the plant and buildings dismantled. Then fifty-three wells were dug to monitor the flow and quality of groundwater, the soil was analysed and either treated to remove grease and heavy metal contaminants or removed for disposal elsewhere, and the population of soil organisms studied to see whether the site could support plants. There can be no doubt that, as other refineries are decommissioned, their sites will be rehabilitated. The principal lesson

from Oakville is that this rehabilitation must be included in the initial planning, and operational procedures modified to make the eventual restoration easier and cheaper.

TRANSPORTING THE OIL

When it has been extracted, oil must be conveyed to the refinery, and the refined products to the factories and communities where they will be used. Transport, too, requires environmental sensitivity, but it can happen that industrial and environmental needs coincide. When it was necessary to convey oil and gas from the fields in the North Slope of Alaska to Prince William Sound in the south the most practical method was to build a pipeline. This could not be buried, for the ground is permanently frozen (permafrost), but nor could it lie on the surface. Had it done so the warmth of the pipe might have melted the surface permafrost. This would have softened the ground beneath the pipeline, possibly causing it to sag and fracture. Damage to the permafrost would also have had adverse ecological consequences. In summer, the surface layer thaws sufficiently for plants to grow, and the plants feed the animals of the region. Were the thaw to become permanent the affected area would turn into a sea of mud, supporting little plant life. So, like many buildings in Alaska, it was mounted on stilts to keep it clear of the ground. The route of the pipeline crossed the migration routes of caribou, large herds of which move seasonally from one feeding ground to another. Were this migration obstructed many caribou would starve. To avoid this the oil companies studied the caribou migration routes and positioned the pipeline high above the ground so the animals could move freely along 'corridors' that pass beneath it. The industry succeeded in conveying its oil and gas and the wildlife of this largely unspoiled region was unharmed.

Coal and oil are no longer taken from the ground with no thought for the environmental consequences. Before work can begin, the operation is planned from start to finish, and it finishes only when the site has been restored to a condition local people find acceptable.

The Trans-Alaska Pipeline at Squirrel Creek crossing. The Pipeline is clear of the ground so it will not damage the permafrost.

CHAPTER 7
POWER

A dinner by candlelight has become part of the human courtship ritual throughout the industrialized world. Merely to invite someone to such an occasion is to suggest romance, an interlude of escape into the privacy of a pool of light too soft to reveal the blemishes and ravages of time written in most of our faces. The invitation also flatters by its generosity, for candlelit dinners have been expensive ever since restaurant owners discovered that turning out the lights justified an increase in their charges. The appeal, not of the romantic occasion but of the circumstances it seems to require, is based at least partly on nostalgia, the opportunity for a brief sojourn in a fancied past where the reality of the harsh present cannot intrude.

ELECTRICITY LIGHTS THE WAY

The illusion cannot be sustained for very long and we do not seek to sustain it. Back home, a flick of a switch turns on the electric light and we would not have it otherwise. Those of us old enough to remember the shadows that menaced and followed as we climbed the stairs to bed, hoping the candle did not blow out before we reached the safety of the covers, would not willingly exchange the switch for the candlestick. Electrification took place quite recently in many rural areas of the industrialized countries, has still not reached some, and, in the less-developed

The lights of the United States at night, as they appear to a satellite 450 nautical miles above the surface.

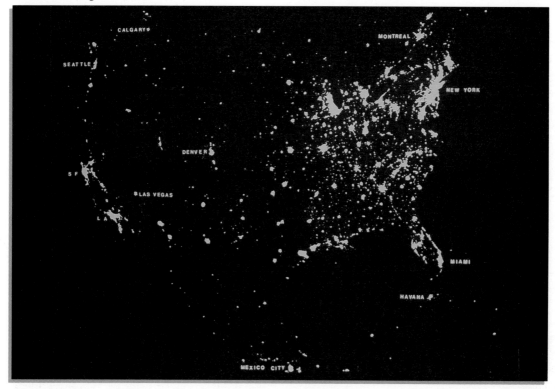

Our demand for electric power is vast, and growing all the time. This is Las Vegas, 47 kilometres (29 miles) west of the Hoover Dam whose generators light its advertising signs.

countries, it is even newer. A symbol of 'modernity', its arrival is welcomed everywhere — as we welcomed it — for the very real benefits it brings.

The proportion of total energy consumed that is delivered as electrical power is increasing in almost every country in the world, and, where it is not increasing, the reason is poverty. There is still a very wide disparity from one country to another in the amount of electricity each person consumes. It is in Norway that consumption is highest, at about 24 000 kilowatt-hours (kWh) for each person each year, compared with less than 6000 kWh per person in Britain, about the same in the USSR, and about 11 000 in both the United States and Luxembourg. At the other end of the scale, annual consumption for each person is only 10 kWh in Chad, 15 in both Burundi and Guinea-Bissau, and 21 in Kampuchea. Between these extremes are the many countries in which electricity consumption will increase as their economies develop.

Most of us think of electricity as it affects us at home, providing lighting, heating, and power to drive domestic appliances, but the greater proportion of electricity consumption takes place in factories. As countries industrialize and increase their electricity consumption, the

Energy can neither be created nor destroyed.

needs of industry must be satisfied first. In the countries that industrialized in the last century, an average of about 70 per cent of electricity is produced for non-residential use. In most of the less industrialized countries the proportion at present exceeds 80 per cent, indicating the extent to which electricity production is likely to expand into the residential sector as soon as economic conditions permit.

Energy can neither be created nor destroyed. When we use it, we merely alter its form, but our ability to do this permits us to choose the form that is most suitable for each application. It is here that electricity scores so highly. We use energy mainly to produce light and heat, and to drive motors. Electricity performs all three tasks extremely well and, so far as the user is concerned, much more conveniently than any alternative. These days we also use it to operate electronic equipment — radio and television production

---

In use, electricity is completely clean.

---

equipment as well as transmitters and receivers, calculators, computers, and the control devices now installed in such everyday items as washing machines and sewing machines. Electronic devices could not use energy in any other form.

Its convenience has made electrical power an important feature of our lives. That convenience arises partly from its immediacy and partly from the ease with which it can be transported. It can be used directly, unlike a fuel that must be burned to produce heat and for many purposes the heat then transformed again into mechanical energy. This immediacy means that its use produces no combustion products or pollutants of any kind whatever. In use, electricity is completely clean. Once generated, it is conveyed to the homes, offices, and factories where it is used by nothing more complicated than a cable. It requires no trucks, no tankers, not even a pipeline.

This immediacy conceals a disadvantage. Electricity cannot be stored. It can be converted into potential chemical energy, in batteries, or kinetic energy, as in a

pumped storage scheme where surplus power at periods of low demand is used to pump water from a low-level reservoir to high-level reservoir, so at times of peak demand the water can be released to produce more power. Such systems are usually cumbersome and expensive. In years to come no doubt they will be improved, especially in the case of batteries, but some such device will always be needed.

PRODUCING THE POWER

Electricity can be generated in a number of ways but, in practice, it is produced by turbine-driven generators. A hollow steel cylinder, called the stator, has insulated copper conductors arranged in groups on its inner surface. More groups of conductors are fixed to the outer surface by a device called the rotor which is mounted on bearings inside the stator. A small generator, called an 'exciter' feeds a direct current into the rotor, making it into an electromagnet, and, when the rotor spins — at about 8000 revolutions per minute — an alternating electric current is generated in the stator conductors. The power to spin the exciter and rotor is provided by turbines, and the turbines may be turned by the movement of air, as in a wind generator, water, as in hydro-electric plants, or by pressurized steam.

HYDRO-ELECTRIC — FOR AND AGAINST

Hydro-electric plants account for a large proportion of the generating capacity in many countries. In Norway, Cameroon, Congo, Costa Rica, and Iceland, for example, almost all electricity is generated in this way, as is more than 90 per cent of Brazil's supply. Small turbines, turned by the flow of a river, can supply an individual household, but generating a public supply, that must provide industrial as well as domestic power, requires much larger installations. In most cases these are based on the damming of a river to make a lake and the controlled release of water from the dam to operate the turbines as it falls.

Such water-generation causes no pollution, but large dams often bring other environmental disadvantages. Technically, a 'large' dam is defined as one more than 150 metres (490 feet) high or whose lake contains more than about 25 billion cubic metres (880 billion cubic feet) of water. The first such dam to be built, in 1936, was the Hoover Dam on the Colorado River in the United States. There was an earthquake while the lake was filling and, since the Hoover was completed, there have been earthquakes in the neighbourhood of, and associated with, at least four other large dams. The water behind the dam weighs billions of tonnes and may be sufficient to cause movement in faulted rocks.

Artificial lakes provide a habitat for many species but, in the seasonal tropics, these species often include parasites part of whose life cycle must be spent in the body of aquatic organisms, usually water snails, and that transmit diseases to humans. The numbers of these parasites are limited naturally by the dry season, during which the intermediate host disappears. The provision of a permanent aquatic habitat can lead to their proliferation and, although the debilitating diseases they bring can be controlled by medicines, and the pests themselves by pesticides, the control is expensive.

There are countries, such as Egypt, where the seasonal flooding of a large river deposits silt, rich in plant nutrient, over the floodplain, thus supplying a natural fertilizer that sustains a traditional system of agriculture. A dam upstream regulates the flow, prevents seasonal flooding and, after a time, farmers on the floodplain find that their soils are depleted and they must begin to buy fertilizers.

Large-scale hydro-electric systems are by no means trouble-free, and there are now grave doubts about the wisdom of

The Aswan High Dam, in Egypt, is 111 metres (364 feet) high and Lake Nasser, behind it, is 500 kilometres (312 miles) long.

Brazilian schemes to build a complex of more than thirty dams in the Amazon Basin. The joint Czechoslovak-Hungarian plan to build a dam complex at Gabcikovo and Nagymaros on the Danube has aroused fierce opposition among Hungarian environmentalists.

FOSSIL FUELS

Hydro-electric schemes are feasible only where a sufficient head of water can be produced. This limits the number of possible sites. Steam-powered generation, on the other hand, suffers no such constraint, and by far the greater proportion of generating plants employ steam-driven turbines. The steam is produced by heating water, and the heat is supplied either by the radioactive decay of uranium or plutonium or, much more commonly, by the burning of a fossil fuel.

When a fuel is burned, the inevitable by-

Electricity is clean and convenient to use but, when it is generated by burning fossil fuels, some pollution is inevitable.

products of combustion may be potentially damaging to the natural environment or to human health. All fossil fuels are based on hydrocarbons, compounds composed principally of carbon and hydrogen. When a pure hydrocarbon is burned, heat is released by the chemical reaction in which the fuel is rapidly oxidized to carbon dioxide and water vapour. These are the two main products. They are not harmful to health, although they are both 'greenhouse gases' and, if the accumulation of such gases in the atmosphere is leading to changes in the global climate, the burning of hydrocarbons must be recognized as the principal cause. Carbon dioxide and water vapour are the sole combustion products, however, only if the fuel is a pure hydrocarbon. If other substances are present, these will also be released.

The purest hydrocarbon fuel is natural gas and, therefore, it is the fuel whose use causes the least environmental harm. Because it is relatively pure, it is also efficient in the sense that the lack of impurities means it produces more heat than other fuels, weight for weight. Petroleum burns less cleanly than natural gas and it often contains sulphur which is emitted as sulphur dioxide, implicated in the acidification of lakes. The solid fuels also contain sulphur, along with a wide range of other impurities, some of which are emitted in gaseous form and some emitted as solid particles or retained with the ash. The potential for environmental pollution from a solid fuel is linked directly to its rank, so that, starting with the most polluting, the order runs: wood, peat, lignite (brown coal), sub-bituminous coal, bituminous coal, anthracite. The severe air pollution in industrial regions of eastern Europe is caused partly by the heavy local dependence on lignite.

CLEANING UP THE FLUE GASES

Most countries now impose strict limits on emissions from industrial plants that burn fossil fuels, and technologies have been developed to prevent those limits being exceeded. Emissions can be reduced either by reducing the amount of fuel used or by extracting pollutants from flue gases before these escape into the atmosphere.

Ash, which may contain heavy metals, is trapped by filters. 'Bag' filters trap particulate matter in much the same way as the bag in a vacuum cleaner, but the very smallest particles, of smoke for example, cannot be held in this way, and to trap them 'electrostatic precipitators' are used. These are devices in which an electric charge of one polarity produces a field

When nitrogen oxides and unburned hydrocarbons, mainly from vehicle exhausts, are trapped beneath a temperature inversion, strong sunlight may cause chemical reactions that produce photochemical smog, seen here in Rio de Janeiro.

that ionizes atoms on the surface of the particles passing through it. A second charge, of opposite polarity, then attracts the charged particles.

The idea is not new. The principle was first described in 1824 by M Hohlfeld, a German mathematics teacher; and the first electrostatic precipitator was installed for pollution control in 1906, at the Selby Smelting factory, near San Francisco.

... the first electrostatic precipitator was installed for pollution control in 1906, ...

Today, there are several types of precipitator, each appropriate to a particular volume and kind of particle, but care must be taken because a high-voltage electrical field can also produce nitrogen oxides and ozone, which are pollutants in their own right.

Sulphur dioxide is removed by 'scrubbers'. The exhaust gases are passed through water containing lime. The sulphur dioxide reacts with the lime (calcium hydroxide) to produce calcium sulphate, an insoluble substance that is left behind as a precipitate. The flue-gas desulphurization process can remove up to 90 per cent of the sulphur dioxide from the gases, reducing the level of emission to one that causes no harm to the environment. The calcium sulphate, chemically identical to naturally occurring gypsum, can be used for the extraction of sulphuric acid or as an ingredient in building materials, although there is some doubt about the potential market for these products because both sulphuric acid and gypsum are in plentiful supply from conventional sources. The lime is produced by quarrying limestone (calcium carbonate), which is then crushed and heated in kilns to drive off carbon dioxide and so convert the carbonate to an oxide (quicklime), which is then converted to the hydroxide by the addition of water (slaking). The large amounts of lime that would be needed if all the fossil-fuel-burning plants in the world were to install flue-gas desulphurization equipment have led some environmentalists to advocate the removal of sulphur from the fuel before it is burned.

Nitrogen oxides, produced during high-temperature combustion by the oxidation of atmospheric nitrogen, are difficult to

---

Nitrogen oxides ... can be controlled by lowering the temperature of combustion.

---

remove from exhaust gases but can be controlled by lowering the temperature of combustion. This can be achieved in modern furnaces that work as 'fluidized beds'. The fuel is pulverized, mixed with an inert substance, and burned in a container through which air is forced under pressure, making the mixture behave as though it were a fluid. This results in much more of the fuel being consumed, so increasing efficiency and reducing emissions, and it operates at a lower combustion temperature. It also allows the processes of fuelling and ash removal to be automated. Ash, which is the final end-product of the combustion of any solid fuel, is retained within the plant until it is sent for final disposal. No way has yet been found to remove carbon dioxide, although a method that produces barium carbonate might be used. Barite (barium sulphate, $BaSO_4$), an ore of barium, is heated to drive off oxygen, yielding a sulphide (BaS); if the sulphide is heated in moist air containing carbon dioxide the reaction yields barium carbonate and hydrogen sulphide ($BaS + H_2O + CO_2 \rightarrow BaCO_3 + H_2S$). The process uses

energy, of course, and leaves hydrogen sulphide for disposal.

IMPROVED EFFICIENCY — COMBINED HEAT AND POWER

Fluidized-bed combustion economizes on fuel, which itself contributes to a reduction in the emission of pollutants, but no more than about 37 per cent of the chemical energy represented by the fuel is converted into useful electrical energy. This low level of efficiency is due to the fact that much of the heat is wasted.

Efficiency can be increased to about 80 per cent if the 'waste' heat can be made to serve a useful purpose, and this has led to increasing interest in combined heat and power (CHP) systems, in which the heat that is inevitably produced but that is not converted into mechanical energy by the turbines is supplied as hot water or steam directly to nearby factories or homes. Again, the idea is not new. The first plant in which steam was produced to be supplied directly to nearby buildings was built in Lockport, New York, in 1877 and, in the years that followed, similar plants were opened in many other cities, especially in the United States, often by companies whose main business was the generation of electricity. The present revival of CHP is widespread and, in

---

Efficiency can be increased to about 80 per cent ...

Britain alone, there are now more than fifty schemes in operation by coal-fired power stations whose combined electrical output is about 1.2 gigawatts [a gigawatt is one billion (thousand million) watts — enough to operate a million one-bar electric fires]. Apart from providing space and water heating, the hot water is valuable in factories that use high-temperature processes because less fuel is needed to achieve the necessary operating temperatures. Water from power stations can also be used to raise the temperature in lagoons to those best suited for the raising of certain species of fish.

Such measures to combat pollution can be taken only where fuel is burned in large amounts. They are essentially industrial measures, feasible only in industrial

---

... electrification ... brings very real environmental benefits.

---

installations. It would be prohibitively expensive, and perhaps technically impossible, to install appropriate equipment in small workshops, far less in private houses. If we are to continue to burn fuels, while at the same time reducing the adverse environmental consequences of doing so, the burning should be concentrated in large plants. This means that, in addition

to being convenient, electrification also brings very real environmental benefits.

THE MIGHTY ATOM

Nuclear power stations also generate heat to operate steam turbines but they burn no fuel, their heat being derived from the radioactive decay of uranium or, in some designs, of plutonium. The heat from the core of the reactor is removed by a coolant that is contained within a sealed system and passed through heat exchangers where it heats the water used to operate the turbines. The uranium oxide 'fuel' is obtained by conventional mining and refining of the ore, uraninite. Plutonium is produced in reactor cores and is obtained by reprocessing, then usually mixed, as plutonium dioxide, with uranium oxide to make 'mixed oxide fuel'. The final waste, consisting of fuel from

Nuclear power stations are usually large, but many believe they have little effect on the environment. This one is at Seal Sands, Teesmouth.

which no more energy can be usefully obtained, is stored for a time, during which it cools, and is then converted into a ceramic product that is sealed in containers for long-term storage where it can remain isolated from the outside environment until its radioactivity has decayed to a level similar to that found in natural uranium-bearing rocks. Depending on the composition of the waste, it must remain isolated for up to 1000 years.

Because no combustion occurs, there are no combustion products and no gaseous or particulate emissions but the coolant becomes contaminated by radioactive substances and care has to be taken to ensure that it cannot escape. Small discharges do occur, nevertheless, but these do not exceed safety limits established by international agreement. Releases into the Irish Sea from waste water outfalls at Sellafield have caused some contamination offshore, but there is no evidence that the contamination has caused harm to any species and, in recent years, the discharges have been greatly reduced. Accidents can also occur, of course, but so far the explosions and fire at Chernobyl were the only accident at a civil reactor to have released a significant amount of radioactive material.

The core of the reactor, which is extremely radioactive, is contained within a shield to prevent workers from exposure. Nuclear power plants emit virtually no contaminants during their normal operation and provide by far the most environmentally benign means for generating electricity on a large scale. Land owned by British Nuclear Fuels, at Sellafield in Cumbria, includes a nature reserve devoted specifically to providing a habitat suitable for the natterjack toad, Britain's most endangered amphibian, which suffered greatly from the acidification, mainly as a result of coal-burning, of the

A man fishing close to the nuclear power station at Chinon, France. It burns no fossil fuel, so the station emits no combustion products and cannot contribute to the greenhouse effect.

sites on which it formerly occurred.

Nuclear power is unpopular in most countries, partly because it is perceived as dangerous. The dangers associated with reactors arise from the large radioactive discharges that may occur in the event of catastrophic failure. There are also economic disadvantages, at least in the short term. Nuclear power plants cost more to build and to decommission than plants which burn fossil fuels but the main expense is incurred in the research and development required for new designs, and can be recouped only where it can be spread among many reactors of similar design. Nevertheless, there are now more than thirty-five countries in which nuclear power contributes to the total electricity supply and, in some, it plays a major part. Belgium produces nearly 70 per cent of its electricity in nuclear reactors, France rather more than 70 per cent, and El Salvador, South Korea, and Taiwan more than 40 per cent. Nuclear power produces more than half of Sweden's electricity, although Sweden is one of several countries that have decided to abandon this technology.

THE FUTURE FOR NUCLEAR POWER

It is possible that the present generation of nuclear reactors, in which the technology is based on the fission of heavy atoms, will be replaced eventually by reactors based on the fusion of light atoms. The development of fusion reactors is now advanced and, by the middle of the next century, they may offer a means of generating electricity from deuterium, or 'heavy hydrogen', and tritium, another form of hydrogen, both obtained initially from sea water.

The future for fusion reactors is still uncertain. What is beyond doubt is that, as industrial development proceeds in the countries of Africa, Asia, and Latin America, the demand for electricity will increase substantially.

Dams

In 1988 there were a total of thirty-two dams more than 150 metres (490 feet) tall under construction in the world as a whole and five more which were lower than 150 metres but whose reservoirs were planned to hold more than 25 billion cubic metres (880 billion cubic feet) of water. The largest capacity was that of the Chapeton dam, on the Paraná river in Argentina. The dam itself was to be only 35 metres (115 feet) high but it would be 224 kilometres (140 miles) long and its reservoir was to hold nearly 61 billion cubic metres (2150 billion cubic feet) of water. It was one of five dams planned for the Paraná.

DAMS — THE CONSEQUENCES

The social and environmental consequences of large hydro-electric schemes are now recognized. Before the Balbina dam reservoir, in the Amazon Basin in Brazil, was filled with 17 billion cubic metres (600 billion cubic feet) of water in 1988, local forest-dwelling Indian people were resettled in places where they were provided with health and educational services. Measures were also taken to minimize the effects on wildlife. Monkeys, anteaters, armadillos, and boas were among about 19 000 animals that were caught and moved to new locations, although there can be no guarantee that such wholesale forced wildlife migration will succeed because the areas receiving the migrants are likely to be either unsuitable or already fully stocked. The Brazilian authorities abandoned another scheme, for the Babaquara dam on the Xingu river, which would have provide 6.5 gigawatts of power but would have involved flooding more than 4000 square kilometres (1545 square miles) of forest.

In Malaysia, however, the 4000 people whose land beside the Rajang river was to

be flooded when the planned 44-billion-cubic-metre (1550-billion-cubic-foot) reservoir for the 200-metre-high (650-foot) Bakun dam was filled were less fortunate. They protested against the resettlement terms they were offered, but work on the project continued.

A major dam is a large engineering project that inevitably causes serious disturbance. Even if its environmental costs are considered acceptable, the loss of land by flooding deprives human communities of their homes and often of the farms that are their means of sustenance. The damming of rivers in the tropics often has disastrous consequences for wildlife. It is hardly surprising that the announcement of a new scheme for a large dam is invariably greeted by protests. Responding to this global concern, in 1988 the World Bank, which is the major funding institution for development projects in the less-developed countries, began to review its funding policies to take more account of their environmental effects and to refuse assistance to those likely to cause serious harm. The rate of dam construction is falling and it seems probable that, in future, less reliance will be placed on major hydro-electric schemes.

By flooding valleys and altering the flow of rivers, large dams can cause serious ecological harm unless they are planned with great care. Below left: A dam in Zambia. Below: The dam at St Maurice à Shawinigan, Québec, is part of a system of dams.

Alternative energy sources

Solar heat is now widely used in passive collectors, fixed to the outsides of buildings, to provide water heating and some space heating. Because they employ solar heat, they are most effective in low latitudes and during summer.

HOT ROCKS

Geothermal energy also supplies heat by exploiting anomalies in the geothermal gradient — the rate at which the temperature of rocks increases with depth. It is obtained either by tapping reservoirs of hot water held in rocks below the ground surface, or by fracturing hot, dry rocks, pumping cold water into them, and extracting the water heated. The technique can work only where a suitable anomaly exists and, in time, the extraction cools the rocks, so exhausting the source. The hot water must be isolated from the surrounding environment for it may contain substances dissolved from the rocks that make it very corrosive.

DIRECT FROM THE SUN

Solar cells use sunlight to generate electricity directly, exploiting the fact that the exposure of certain substances to light causes a flow of electrons. Developed for use in space, the initial high cost and low efficiency of solar cells have been improved greatly. A large area of cells is required to produce useful amounts of electricity but, in years to come, they may contribute to supplies in large buildings, and, because the technology uses light rather than heat, it is suitable for use in high latitudes and in winter — although focusing lenses may be needed to increase the intensity of the light.

SEA POWER

A tidal barrage — a 'barrage' is a dam — is a type of hydroelectric installation that uses the tidal flow of water to operate turbines. A large tidal movement is required, limiting the number of suitable sites. Incoming water is allowed to pass and is then retained behind the dam to be released later in a controlled fashion. Depending on the design, the turbines may be turned by the ebb tide only or by both flow and ebb tides. By interrupting the natural flow of water, tidal barrages may interfere with sedimentation processes, causing serious ecological effects, especially to estuarine birds and in some cases to fisheries.

Wave-power uses the vertical movement of waves to generate electricity. In some designs, devices floating at the surface are rocked by the waves; in others, the wave motion causes oscillations in columns of water held in devices on the sea bed. The installations must be large to produce useful amounts of power; they can be sited only where the average amplitude of waves is large, and they must be able to withstand storms.

FARMING THE WIND

Electricity is generated from wind power by the rotation of blades, essentially similar to aircraft propellers, mounted on tall vertical towers, and sited on high ground reliably exposed to wind. Useful in providing a domestic power supply to remote communities, a 'wind farm' must consist of at least 1500 generators if it is to match the output of one conventional power station. The site is very large indeed because the generators must be widely separated to prevent them from 'shading' one another. This, and the noise the generators produce, mean that proposals to build wind farms are usually opposed by local communities and are appropriate only where large, unpopulated spaces are available. No-one knows whether interference in the flow of air may produce meteorological or other effects downwind.

Left: *Solar panels in Andalucia, Spain, where the sunlight is sufficiently intense for them to make a useful contribution to energy supplies.* Below: *It takes at least 1500 wind generators to match the output of a conventional power station, so 'wind farms' are very large. This one is near Palm Springs, California.*

CHAPTER 8
MINERALS AND MATERIALS

The paper on which this book is printed is made from wood pulp. In the old game of 'animal, vegetable, or mineral?' most people would classify it as 'vegetable'. This is approximately true, but only approximately. The wood fibres provide a basic structure for the paper that is strengthened by the addition of a filler. The filler also makes the paper whiter. 'Art' paper, which has a very white, shiny surface and is used for printing high-quality illustrations, is coated with a layer of the same substance. The substance is kaolin, or china clay, and it is a mineral.

THE HARMLESS FILLER

The name 'kaolin' is from *kao ling*, the Chinese for 'high ridge'. The mineral was

A china clay pit in Cornwall. The high-pressure hose washes the clay from the rock matrix to form a slurry from which it is then separated.

first mined at a hill near the city of Fouli-ang, in south-east China, and was used in the manufacture of fine porcelain. Europeans first learned of it in the late seventeenth century. Deposits were then discovered in France and Saxony, in south-west England by William Cookworthy in 1764, and, since then, in Bohemia, Spain, the USSR, Brazil, and in several parts of the United States. Apart from paper manufacture, which now provides 80 per cent of the total market, and porcelain accounting for 12 per cent, china clay is used in the rubber, plastics, paint, ink, cosmetic, and pharmaceutical industries. When you take a white tablet, such as an aspirin, a minute amount of the drug is dispersed in an inert, harmless filler, and the filler is china clay. About 15 million tonnes of china clay are produced annually in the world as a whole, about 3 million tonnes of it in south-west England.

THE FLINT TRADE

China clay is a mineral, technically defined as a naturally occurring, inorganic, solid substance that has a characteristic chemical composition. Minerals are often crystalline but not always so. Rocks are composed of minerals. Minerals must be extracted from the ground and, more loosely, the term is often applied to any substance obtained by mining or quarrying. The very first human industry, which dominated economies long before the introduction of farming and for some time afterwards, was based on a mineral. Flint, which a skilled worker can break into flakes with very sharp edges, was used to make a wide variety of cutting tools and weapons. When people learned to work metals, flint gave way to iron and the Stone Age became the Iron Age, but by then flint had been in use for hundreds of thousands of years.

Flint is made from silica — silicon dioxide — the same compound as quartz and sand. It formed in sediments on the sea bed when silica filled spaces made by animal burrows and by the decomposition of the soft parts of sponges and other animals that were mixed with chalk from the crushed remains of animal shells. It occurs today as bands and nodules in chalk and, although it can be found lying at the surface, there was a time when the best industrial flints were mined from the chalk. Flint tools were superior to those made from most other stones and, because the mineral occurs only in certain places, it became a valuable item of trade.

Grimes Graves and the area surrounding them in eastern England are remains of an industrial site. Several vertical shafts

ancient flint mines are ... tiny compared with the largest of modern mineral mines.

descend to a main pit, at a depth of about 12 metres (40 feet), from which twenty-seven horizontal galleries extend to form an intricate network of tunnels. The larger galleries are just big enough for two men to pass each other. In the smaller ones, miners — possibly skilled professionals — lay prostrate to prize out the flints. The waste material excavated to open the mines was dumped outside, and surrounding woodland was cleared, probably to provide farmland where food was grown to support what must have been a prosperous community.

STONE GIVES WAY TO METALS

Metals are obtained either by mining them in their pure form, as 'native' metals, or by extracting them from their 'ores' — the compounds in which they occur naturally in rocks. Gold usually occurs in the native form, though often

Some mines are very deep. At the East Driefontein Gold Mine, in the Transvaal, South Africa, these men are working 1952 metres (6400 feet) below ground level.

containing other metals as impurities, and copper sometimes does, but most metals occur as ores. In either case they are classed as minerals, and modern mining is a large-scale operation.

The ancient flint mines are impressive, but they are tiny compared with the largest of modern mineral mines. Around Witwatersrand, in South Africa, there are gold mines extending to depths of more than 3400 metres (11 150 feet), and the mines at Butte, Montana, are about 1600 metres (5250 feet) deep with more than 5500 kilometres (3400 miles) of passages extending over an area of some 5 square kilometres (2 square miles). The mines of the St Joseph Lead Company in Missouri are so extensive they are served by two underground machine shops nearly 10 kilometres (16 miles) apart, one covering 2.2 hectares (5$\frac{1}{2}$ acres) and the other 1.5 hectares (3$\frac{3}{4}$ acres), where underground machinery is repaired and some of the machines are built. Where deposits lie close to the ground surface they are mined by open-pit methods, like opencast coal mines but sometimes larger. At Bingham, Utah, for example, there is an open-cut copper mine that measures 3.2 kilometres (almost 2 miles) across the rim and nearly 900 metres (2950 feet) deep, forming a stadium-like area that is said to be large enough to hold the entire population of New York City.

Coal occurs in discrete formations as the pure material. Its quality varies but the coal in a seam is not mixed with other substances. Minerals, on the other hand, and especially metalliferous ores, are dispersed among rocks with which they form an intimate mixture. The quality, or 'grade', of a mineral is measured as the proportion of it that can be extracted from the rocks where it occurs.

Metal ores usually contain fairly high concentrations of the metal. Cuprite, for example, contains 88.8 per cent copper and chalcocite contains 79.9 per cent. Both are important ores for copper. Uraninite, the most important uranium ore, contains between 45 and 60 per cent uranium depending on the form the ore mineral takes. Iron is mined from ores containing about 55 per cent down to about 25 per cent of iron. These high figures are misleading, however, because of the way the ore is dispersed. An ore grade of 80 per cent copper may mean the metal is dispersed in the rocks containing the ore at a concentration of no more than 8 to 16 per cent, and, when prices are high, copper can be mined down to about 5 per cent. A uraninite content of, say, 50 per cent means in practice that the uranium-bearing rocks contain from 0.01 per cent to 0.2 per cent of uranium oxide. Hematite, magnetite, limonite, and siderite, the principal ores of iron, occur in large, fairly pure deposits.

In open-pit mines, explosives are used to shatter rocks which are then crushed and processed to extract their metals. This blast is taking place at a mine at Kanoto, Zaire.

Whether or not an ore can be mined depends on the value of the mineral, its location, and the technology available for its extraction. Minerals that command high prices, such as uranium, gold, and some precious stones, most notably diamonds, can be mined profitably at low grades and in remote places where the cost of moving in equipment and workers is high. Less valuable minerals, such as iron, which is used in large amounts but is fairly common, can be mined economically only in reasonably accessible sites and at high grades. The economic determinants are far from fixed. A change in the rate of industrial activity can lead to shortages or surpluses of particular minerals, so raising or lowering prices and opening new mines or closing old ones. An advance in mining technology can make it possible to extract minerals at grades that were previously uneconomical.

The possibility of such changes, holding as it does the promise that uneconomical but unexhausted workings may one day open again, renders many mines marginal, and owners are reluctant to abandon them altogether if closure can be avoided.

Molten gold being poured at the West Driefontein Gold Mine.

Open-pit mines can occupy large areas. This is Mount Newman Mine, at Pilbara, Western Australia, which produces iron ore.

In the case of workings deep below ground, this often requires that some activity be continued, at the very least the operation of the pumps that prevent galleries from flooding, for it may be impossible to remove all the water and make the galleries safe again in a badly flooded mine. Open-pit workings, however, must usually be closed and the land restored.

CHINA CLAY — BOTTOMLESS PITS

The exception to this rule is the china clay extraction industry where primary deposits are being worked. A primary deposit is one that formed in the place where it is found. A secondary deposit formed in one place but was then moved — by natural movements of the Earth's crust or transported by water — to the place where it is found. Some china clay, for example in Georgia in the United States, is mined from secondary deposits but, in Britain, the deposits are primary.

They formed from below, about 300 million years ago, soon after the collision between two land masses caused folding in sedimentary rocks accompanied by fracturing through which molten rock was exuded from below the Earth's crust. The molten rock solidified to form granite but, while it was still molten hot, acid fluids moving upwards through it penetrated cracks. Where these fluids encountered sodium-rich feldspars, a constituent of the granite, they reacted with it, producing china clay. This means not only that the deposits are to all intents and purposes bottomless but, in many cases, the quality of the clay improves with depth. The clay is extracted from the quartz sand and mica with which it is mixed by water, fired at the material under high pressure, and is removed as a slurry. The economic limit to extraction is determined mainly by the cost of lifting the slurry and the waste material to ground level. Each time a technological innovation makes this task easier, work may be resumed at an old pit that had become uneconomically deep.

Open-pit workings of this kind are sometimes likened to opencast coal pits but the resemblance is superficial. When

Eventually, the iron ore in this open-pit mine will be exhausted and the mine will close. Modern good mining practice requires that the site will then be restored, for amenity, agricultural, or some other use decided by the local community.

A high-pressure hose, called a 'monitor', blasting china clay from the surrounding granite in Cornwall. The quality of the clay improves with depth, making it impractical to back-fill the pit.

the coal has been removed from an opencast pit, there is no reason to postpone filling in the site and restoring the landscape, but there is every reason to keep open a china clay pit over a primary deposit, although it is often used to store water, of which large amounts are used. As a pit grows deeper, it must also grow wider to maintain a safe and stable angle of slope at the sides, and a pit may have to be abandoned and filled if its further expansion is impossible because adjacent land is being used for other purposes.

The reluctance to abandon pits affects the way in which waste material is deposited. Ideally, waste tips should not be built in places that might be mined in the future, for the tips would effectively sterilize the mineral deposit. This constraint does not apply to underground mines, which can be extended by tunnelling beneath their own tips, but the combination of pits kept open for future use and waste tips made on nearby land not designated for mining means the open-pit mining of primary deposits often occupies rather large areas.

There is no longer any need for mine waste simply to be dumped. Some is made into banks to screen the mining area, some may find other uses, for example, as building or road-making material, and the tips made from the remainder can be

Land reclamation around china clay workings

For every tonne of china clay that is produced, there are about 4.5 tonnes of overburden, 3.5 tonnes of sand, and 1 tonne of micaceous residue — a white, putty-like material left behind after processing. In Cornwall, the china clay industry produces about 24 million tonnes of wastes a year. At one time, it was simply dumped, some of it in rivers.

Today English China Clays has developed disposal methods that, within a few years, produce an apparently natural, well-vegetated landscape.

Each type of waste is disposed of separately. The overburden and sand are deposited separately, some of the overburden in tips and some to build dams behind which the micaceous mate-

rial is held in 'lagoons' until it dries. The dams are raised as the level behind them rises.

The tips, made from almost pure, white sand, are built in a long, flat-topped shape, up to 24 metres (almost 80 feet) high and, as one 'lift' is completed, another is built

China clay extraction creates a landscape of white hills and valleys, with brilliantly blue lakes.

on top of it. The material drains freely and the tip is prone to erosion by water and by wind. The sand contains little nutrient and is not readily colonized by plants.

Reclamation begins as soon as a 'lift' is complete. Seeds of three or four species of grasses and two or three species of legumes, together with fertilizer and a mulch made from waste paper, all mixed in water, are sprayed from tankers on to the sides of the tips.

A NEW ROLE FOR SOAY SHEEP

As soon as the vegetation is established and growing strongly, Soay sheep are allowed on to the tip sides. Light, agile, and independent, the sheep crop the grasses closely, which encourages their growth, and they fertilize the pasture with their droppings. Later, shrubs are planted and eventually trees. In a few years the waste tips

are converted into wooded hills.

The mica lagoons, and the dams surrounding them, are also planted and grazed. After a few years, they become either permanent pasture or potential arable land. Potatoes, winter wheat, and a

The reclaimed waste tips are 'managed' by hardy, sure-footed Soay sheep. Once an endangered breed, their future was assured when English China Clays developed a large flock.

range of vegetables have been grown successfully on them.

The overburden tips have gentler slopes than the sand tips and, where possible, topsoil is added as the uppermost layer. This makes planting easier and they become scrub and woodland more quickly.

Based on years of research, the reclamation of these unpromising materials has led to the development of specialized equipment as well as techniques. A version of a road-surfacing machine, laying china clay waste and grass seed rather than asphalt, has been used to provide tennis courts and playing fields in nearby villages.

The slurry is pumped into tanks where the clay and water begin to separate.

... *tips often become havens for wildlife.*

seeded as soon as they are completed. The resulting hills are artificial, but they look natural because, after a time, they are covered by natural vegetation. Because their sides are too steep to be cultivated and the tips are on land owned by the mining company to which there is no public access, such seeded and recolonized tips often become havens for wildlife.

CLEANING UP THE METALS INDUSTRIES

The ease with which mine waste can be converted into useful habitat depends on its content. China clay waste is not toxic but waste from metal mining may be. Metals seldom occur in isolation, and those that are not required, together with small amounts of the desired metal, form part of the waste. They are often

poisonous to plants, the waste tips may remain bare for a long time, and, in the past, local watercourses were often polluted by chemicals draining from the tips. These days mine wastes must be stored in such a way as to prevent them from causing pollution, and many rivers have recovered. The best mining practice demonstrates the extent to which improvement is possible and, in countries where less emphasis has been placed on environmental protection, there is now strong pressure for reform.

Tips do not remain bare for ever, even so. Strains of certain grasses, plantains, catchflies, and other plants have evolved a tolerance, some for one metal, some for another, and eventually tips do become colonized to an extent. In some places where mining ceased long ago, it now takes an expert eye to identify the waste tips.

Iron is extracted from its ore by smelting. It was the smelting of iron and its subsequent processing into steel that once lit up the night skies and darkened the day skies of areas dependent on the iron and steel industries. Other metals are extracted partly by chemical means. The froth flotation method, for example, involves grinding the ore to a fine powder, mixing it thoroughly with water to which chemical reagents have been added, then agitating the mixture vigorously. The reagents have an affinity for the desired metal and a froth forms in which the metal tends to adhere to the surface of the bubbles while the waste settles to the bottom. The froth is skimmed from the surface and the metal extracted from it. The sediment, which still contains some of the useful metal, is mixed with other chemicals that function as fluxes and then smelted to separate the residue of metal from the waste.

The metal industries generally were once a major source of environmental pollutants, but today their impact on the environment is much reduced. The improvement has come about partly through the installation of filters to retain particulate matter, precipitators to collect fine dust and smoke, scrubbers to remove sulphur dioxide formerly emitted when sulphide ores were smelted, but partly through technological advances in the industries themselves. Electricity has replaced the burning of solid fuels in

By polluting rivers and clearing natural forest, insensitive mining can still cause serious environmental damage. This tin mine is in the Amazon Basin, in Brazil.

Old industrial sites reclaimed

From 1850 until 1949 Lazenby Bank in the county of Cleveland was the site of the most productive iron ore mines in the region. The mining industry fed the growing iron and steel industry which stimulated other industries, and together these

Once the site of iron ore mines, Lazenby Bank, Cleveland, has been restored and is now a nature reserve, rich in wildlife and very popular with local people. The factory in the background is the ICI Wilton Works.

developments provided the basis for the growth and prosperity of Middlesbrough. Mining ceased when the two ironstone seams were exhausted. Today Lazenby Bank is a country park, living evidence of the way an area of countryside can be helped to recover from the ravages of an industrial past and acquire new value as a popular public amenity.

A NEW LEASE OF LIFE

In 1988, ICI leased the 89-hectare (222-acre) area to Cleveland County Council together with the school house in a nearby village, which is to become a field studies centre. Sensitive management and natural regeneration have turned the Bank into a place rich in wildlife while preserving remind-

A conservation area in the Lazenby Bank nature reserve, where an open-canopy, mixed, broadleaved woodland is developing.

A VARIETY OF WILDLIFE

The diversity of plants encourages a wide range of animals. There are roe deer, foxes, moles, stoats, weasels, and hedgehogs, and more than eighty species of birds have been recorded. Wood warblers and willow warblers, blackcap and garden warblers breed at Lazenby Bank, and, in some years, there are also redstarts and tree pipits. There are woodcocks, spotted flycatchers, great spotted woodpeckers, and, though less common, green woodpeckers. The moorland supports different birds, such as meadow pipits and grasshopper warblers, and the ponds and wetland areas of the Park provide habitat for frogs, toads, smooth newts, and dragonflies. There are many species of butterflies and moths.

ers of its history. Visitors are excluded from a few areas but most of the Bank accessible, with well-signposted footpaths and car parking.

The Guibal Fanhouse, now a listed building, remains, as does the tramway along which its coal was delivered. The Fanhouse once held the steam-driven fan that drew foul air from the mines. The tramway, running right through the Park, forms the main path. There are older sites, too, including two Bronze Age burial mounds and an Iron Age hill fort, on Eston Nab, a 242-metre (794-foot) hill with commanding views of the Pennines and the Durham coast.

Many of the old waste tips have been colonized by gorse and broom, and elsewhere the vegetation consists mainly of woodland. The broadleaved species include silver birch, sweet chestnut, wych elm, and beech, with elder and hazel, and there is a conifer plantation with larch and Corsican pine. The top of Eston Nab has a typical moorland vegetation. There are many flowering herbs, some of them rare.

Fly agaric (Amanita muscaria) *fungus growing in Lazenby Bank. It occurs beneath birch and pine trees.*

Unless emissions are controlled, steel making can cause serious air pollution. This is Shanghai Steel Works.

many operations, so reducing combustion emissions, and processing is much more efficient. The economics of the modern world dictate that industries cannot survive unless they work efficiently, and an increase in efficiency implies better use of the raw material to obtain more value from it. If more of the raw material is used, less waste is produced. Although it is expensive to install equipment to prevent pollution, the investment is often repaid in higher output and lower operating costs.

MINING WITH BACTERIA

New extraction methods are increasing efficiency, and reducing the potential for pollution, still further. Some years ago, it was discovered that, when metals begin to seep from waste tips, they are sometimes being released by bacteria inside the tip. *Thiobacillus ferroxidans*, for example, extracts the sulphur it needs from sul-

phide compounds and releases the metal as a soluble oxide. It can release liquid containing fifty parts per million of recoverable copper and it oxidizes iron in the same way. This offers the possibility of recovering metals from old waste tips and from low-grade ores. It may even allow metals to be extracted from inaccessible rocks without cutting or crushing them. A solution containing a culture of the appropriate bacterium is sprayed on to the rock, ore, or waste, and the metal recovered from the liquor that drains away. Copper is being extracted by bacterial leaching in several United States mines, and the possibilities are being explored in several European countries. In 1974 the Western Mining Corporation of Western Australia announced that it had discovered a way to use bacteria to recover nickel. In Portugal, bacterial leaching has been used since 1953 to recover uranium from rocks without cutting into them, and some uranium mines in Canada and other countries also use the technique. It can also be used to mine gold.

RECYCLING AND REPLACEMENT

Demand for new metal can be reduced by recycling. Almost all the scrap produced in the course of smelting or manufacture, as well as a proportion of used metal, is recycled. Recycling could contribute more, although it can be difficult and expensive to separate individual metals from articles that are made from more than one.

The trend, however, is towards the replacement of metals altogether in an increasing number of products. For many years, the principal use for mercury was in switchgear, the heavy duty switches used in factories. Such switches have now been replaced by electronic devices, and mercury switches are no longer required. Most copper was used in electrical wiring,

Right: A collection point in Italy, for wastes that will be recycled.
Below: These pans, on sale in a Brazilian market, were made from old tin cans.

and especially in submarine telegraph and telephone cables. Information is now transmitted between continents as radio waves beamed to and from satellites. The submarine cables are no longer needed. Elsewhere, aluminium wiring has been used as a cheaper alternative to copper, and now metal wires are being replaced by optical fibres, made from glass.

Reinforced with synthetic resins, glass fibre is used instead of wood to make small boats, and instead of mild steel to make the bodies of some small cars. Resin-reinforced carbon fibres are lighter and stronger than steel, immune to rust, and may eventually replace steel in car bodies. Even engines may one day be made from ceramic materials rather than from metal.

Ceramics are made by forming a natural mineral, such as a clay, into a required

---

... engines may one day be made from ceramic materials ...

---

shape and then heating it strongly enough to cause vitrification, in which individual crystals lose their structure and fuse. The result is a hard, impermeable material. This is the way pots are made, and the underlying technique is as old as knowledge of pottery itself.

CHIPS, RESINS, AND CERAMICS

It was the space programme and the electronics industry that, between them, stimulated new interest in this ancient technology. Modern electronics are based on the concept of the semiconductor, a crystalline material in which the electrical conductivity is intermediate between that of a conductor and an insulator. The substance that is now most widely used in semiconductors is silicon, produced as a

single crystal that is cut into small wafers to make 'chips'. 'Chip' production is counted as a branch of the advanced ceramics industry and, in 1987, it earned an estimated $2.2 billion in the United States alone. The development of space vehicles called for materials able to withstand extreme temperatures and stresses. Advanced ceramics were devised to meet the demand, and they have now found other outlets in engine components, cutting tools, heat exchangers, and for making industrial machine parts that must resist corrosion and wear. This branch of the industry earned an estimated $4.4 billion in 1987, and is growing fast.

Synthetic resins are made from organic chemicals, derived mainly from petroleum, although they could be obtained from coal. Glass in its various forms and other ceramics are made from common minerals, and resins and ceramics are extremely economical in their use of materials. To appreciate just how economical, you need only compare the valves and metal wiring in a pre-war radio receiver with the miniaturized printed circuits in a modern radio. These new materials are used as substitutes for metals not because they are cheaper, although they often are, but because they are superior.

They are also cleaner to make. Their manufacture takes place in modern factories using new, efficient plant. Provided due care is taken with the process chemicals used, they have little effect on the surrounding environment.

The materials industries were a major source of pollution throughout the Industrial Revolution. The pollutants have been identified and ways found to prevent their release, or even to exploit them as with bacterial leaching, and today the mining and processing of minerals cause little harm in many places. The substitution of new materials for metals represents a further advance, in technology and in environmental protection.

How blue is the Danube?

Pollutants do not respect international frontiers. Polluted air may be carried long distances by weather systems, and rivers that cross continents transport downstream the accumulated wastes discharged into them as they pass through densely populated regions. Reducing such 'transfrontier' pollution requires the agreement of all the countries involved. The Danube, the most important river in central and south-eastern Europe, is managed by ten countries. The European Convention on the Protection of International Watercourses Against Pollution, produced by the Council of Europe in 1975, is intended to help regulate the management of major river basins, such as that of the Danube.

FROM BLACK FOREST TO BLACK SEA

The Danube is is about 2800 kilometres (1740 miles) long, drains about 820 000 square kilometres (317 000 square miles), and passes through eight countries. It rises in the mountains of the Black Forest, in West Germany, and, near Regensburg, it is linked to the Rhine and Main by a canal. Then it passes through Austria, Czechoslovakia, Hungary, Yugoslavia, Roma-

nia, and Bulgaria before it discharges into the Black Sea, in the USSR. Its delta, covering about 2600 square kilometres (1000 square miles), is a region of swamps and reed marshes interspersed with isolated, wooded hills. The Black Sea Nature Reserve, in the Ukraine, part of an internationally important wetland covering 1038 square kilometres (400 square miles) of the delta, contains 595 species of plants and 280 species of nesting, wintering, and migrating birds.

The Danube is also linked to the Black Sea by a canal from Romania, opened in

The Danube, one of Europe's longest rivers, rises in Germany and flows through eight countries before it ends at the Black Sea. All the countries bordering it use it for commercial transport and recreation. It is seen here near Visgard, in Yugoslavia.

1984. In 1980 the Bulgarian and Romanian Governments agreed to divert the river as part of the Turnu Magurele-Nikopol hydro-electric complex. At Gabcikovo in Czechoslovakia and Nagymaros in Hungary, work started in 1978 on a hydro-electric scheme that would divert the main navigational channel and redirect 25 kilometres ($15^1/_2$ miles) of the river and its bayous through a concrete channel. The scheme has aroused fierce opposition from Hungarian environmentalists, who fear the damage caused would include the flooding of the 'Danube Bend', a popular resort area for the people of Budapest. The river is navigable by special river craft for most of its length, and all states may use it freely. Pleasure boats and barges use it as a highway, and small sea-going vessels can enter its lower reaches. Bauxite, the principal ore for aluminium production, is carried from Hungary to the USSR, and iron ore from the USSR to Hungary and Czechoslovakia, as well as grain and Romanian oil. Vulnerable to pollution from spilled cargoes, it is fed by 300 or more tributaries, some of them large rivers, and passes through Vienna, Bratislava, Budapest, and so on.

CHAPTER 9
CHEMICALS

Take a fat or oil, of animal or vegetable origin, add caustic soda, boil the mixture, and, after a time, add ordinary salt; gradually the material will separate into two layers. The bottom layer consists of a mixture of glycerol and salty water. The upper layer is soap. Until the beginning of the last century, most Americans made their soap in this way, at home, using a method little different from the one the Romans used — they boiled tallow, caustic soda, and wood ash, with added salt. That they gave up domestic soap-making and began to buy their soap from shops is due very largely to one man, a French chemist called Nicolas Leblanc (1742-1806).

Some time in the late eighteenth century, the French Academy of Sciences offered a prize to anyone who could find a way to make alkali in large quantities cheaply. This is what Leblanc succeeded in doing, some authorities say in 1783 others in 1790 or 1791. He invented a process for making 'soda ash', or 'washing soda' — chemically sodium carbonate — which could be used as a substitute for caustic soda in soap making. As raw materials Leblanc used sodium chloride (common salt), sulphuric acid, coke, and calcium carbonate (limestone). The salt was heated with sulphuric acid to produce sodium sulphate; then the sodium sulphate was heated with coke and limestone to produce sodium carbonate, calcium sulphide, and carbon dioxide. The mixture was dissolved in water and the sodium carbonate extracted by crystallization.

The significance of this invention lay in the fact that Leblanc set out from the start with the intention that the process should work efficiently and economically on an industrial scale. It was very successful, although Leblanc gained little from it. He opened his own factory but it was confiscated during the French Revolution, as were his patents and, so far as anyone knows, he never collected his prize. Napoleon gave him back his factory but by then he could not afford to open it and, in the end, he committed suicide. The Leblanc process is rarely used today, but it marked the beginning of the chemical industry and its story remains typical of the way the industry operates.

SMOKESTACKS ON THE SCENE

Alkali-makers used sulphuric acid, so rather than buying it, they began to make it for themselves, some by burning sulphur, others by burning pyrites — the sulphide of copper or iron. Burning a metal sulphide leaves a sulphate as a by-product, and copper sulphate and ferrous sulphate could be sold, and were. React salt with sulphuric acid, which is the first stage in the Leblanc process, and one of the products is hydrochloric acid. In the early days, this was released through the factory chimney and it killed any plant with which it came into contact. James Muspratt (1793-1886) sought to reduce the pollution by making the chimney taller, and thus invented the familiar smokestack — his were 90 metres (295 feet) high. The tall chimney merely dispersed the acid over a wider area, of course, but then it was discovered that, if the gas is passed through a tower packed with coke over which water is trickled, the acid is removed as a liquid that can be collected.

It was ingenious but it did not solve the pollution difficulty because there was no demand for hydrochloric acid. For a time it was dumped at sea. This was clearly unsatisfactory, not least because it was wasteful, and so it remained until another discovery was made. If hydrochloric acid is reacted with manganese dioxide, chlorine is produced. Chlorine reacted with calcium hydroxide (slaked lime) makes bleaching powder, which was marketed very profitably. There was still a waste product, of course, this time manganese chloride. Then two things happened. The first was the invention of a way to recover the manganese from the chloride so it could be used over and over again; the second was a way to produce chlorine from hydrochloric acid without using manganese at all. In the end a way was found even to recover the surplus sulphur from the waste of the alkali factories.

THE CHEMICAL INDUSTRY BRANCHES OUT

In 1856, when he was an eighteen-year old student at the Royal College of Chemistry, in London, William Henry Perkin (1838-1907) spent his Easter vacation experimenting in the laboratory he had made for himself at home. He was trying to make quinine (the drug used to treat malaria) from coal tar which he obtained from the local gas works. Coal tar contains benzene from which aniline can be obtained, a colourless, oily liquid. Perkin treated an aniline salt with potassium dichromate, hoping to produce crystals of quinine. Instead all he made was a black, tarry liquid into which, for no apparent reason, he dropped a piece of silk cloth. When he removed the cloth, it

Chemical factories can be made more attractive by sensitive landscaping and the use of trees for screening. This is an ICI Formulation plant in Nicaragua.

These long, low, fairly unobtrusive buildings house an ICI factory in Ghana.

was a beautiful mauve colour. He had made the first synthetic dye. He abandoned his studies, opened a factory, grew rich and famous, and was knighted. Not only had he synthesized a dye, he had launched an entirely new branch of the chemical industry, based on organic compounds — those that are based on carbon.

Until then there had been little use for coal tar but now it became a valuable material and was no longer permitted to escape in the smoke from industrial coal-burning. As the years passed, it developed

---

... industrialists do not wish to injure their workers — or themselves ...

---

as the base for thousands of useful compounds — the development of which marked the start of what is now the vast industry engaged in synthesizing chemical compounds — but the search for still more compounds led chemists in the direction of petroleum. Around 1920, petroleum became the raw material for the production of isopropyl alcohol; other products followed, and petrochemicals formed one more branch of the chemical industry.

Throughout their history, chemical manufacturers have begun by devising a process that will employ chemical reactions to transform raw materials into a chemical compound for which there is a commercial market. The process must work reliably on a large scale, for what succeeds in a laboratory may fail when flasks and beakers are replaced by tanks and vats in a factory. In addition, it must not be so costly that the final product is too expensive to sell. Chemistry, industrial engineering, and economics are intimately intertwined. The process must also be safe. The raw materials, end product, and the intermediate products that never leave the factory may be poisonous, corrosive, or flammable, and their secure containment and control have to be incorporated in the design of the plant. This is obvious common sense, for industrialists do not wish to injure their workers — or themselves — and there is no profit to be made from a factory that is destroyed.

The next step is to economize on the cost of raw materials. This may involve finding cheaper sources, or cheaper alternatives, but very often it has led manufacturers to begin further back in the operation, and make their own feedstocks from simpler raw materials. It is not long before one process leads to others — as, for example, when the alkali-makers ceased to buy expensive sulphuric acid and took to making their own from cheap pyrite. With a new process and new plant in which to conduct it, the factory grows larger.

Then the search begins to find uses for the waste products. Sometimes raw materials can be extracted from them for use within the existing factory, as when manganese was recovered from the chlorine-making process. Or the wastes can become raw materials for an entirely new process, with a different marketable product, in the way that waste hydrochloric acid was used to make bleach. More

... *uses for waste products* ...

processes and products are added, and the factory grows larger again.

It is not surprising that, after a generation or two, what began as a modest factory making one product has become a vast industrial complex making many. Nor is it surprising to discover that an industry whose need to progress is built into its history and structure invests more than most in research and development. This produces great flexibility and there are often several ways to make a particular product, but the great rate of progress carries the risk that a process may be obsolete by the time it completes its development, so there is always a great sense of urgency.

FAMILIAR GOODS FROM CHEMICALS

Few of the products of the chemical industry reach the public directly. Most are used as the raw materials in the making of other goods. Around the home we use soap, of course, and various cleaning fluids, but we may be unaware of the fact that many familiar items actually owe their existence to industrially produced chemicals. All of our synthetic fibres, for example, begin in chemical factories, as do most of our synthesized materials. The industry supplies our dyes, paints, plastics, cushion fillings, insulation materials, and adhesives. Modern plywood is made from thin sheets of wood, but the glue that bonds them together was made in a chemical factory. The industry provides the materials to make our pens, inks, long-playing records, and recording tapes, and, of course, the fuel and lubricants for our cars.

Other chemical products are still less obvious. The production of agricultural chemicals has increased food production throughout the world, and has made food cheaper than it would be otherwise. The drugs and medicines we use are made by

Aëdes aegypti, seen here feeding on a human, is the mosquito that transmits yellow fever. It occurs widely in the tropics and subtropics but can be controlled with insecticides.

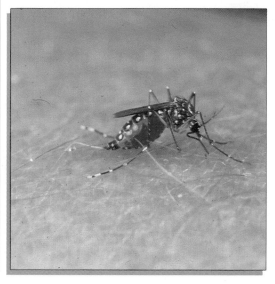

Lake Magadi

Although much of the world's soda ash is produced industrially, it does occur naturally in some places and can be extracted. For more than sixty years the Magadi Soda Company has been taking soda ash from Lake Magadi, southwest of Nairobi, Kenya. The Lake, with a surface area of about 80 square kilometres (31 square miles), lies in the lowest part of the Rift Valley, one of the most delicate of all areas of natural habitat. The region around the Lake is dry, very warm, and the vegetation is sparse.

Alkaline springs feed water into the Lake but there is no outlet. Water is lost through evaporation, and sodium sesquicarbonate, with some sodium fluoride and sodium sulphate, settle out from the saturated water to form thick lake-bed deposits of material called 'trona'. This is removed by dredging, crushed on board the dredgers, mixed with lake water and pumped ashore as a slurry for calcining (kilning) in the factory. The factory produces about 300 000 tonnes of soda ash and about 40 000 tonnes of salt a year.

FOOD FOR FLAMINGOES

This large industrial operation, with a town associated with the factory, has had little or no effect on wildlife. Not much can survive in the alkaline conditions of the Lake, but *Spirulina*, thrives. This genus of cyanobacterium, which forms long, curling filaments, feeds one species of fish — *Oreochromis alcalicus* — and large numbers of a few species of invertebrates, and these in turn provide food for many species of birds. There is also a large population of flamingoes, mainly lesser flamingoes (*Phoenicopterus minor*), which feed on the *Spirulina* itself. Egrets and herons, white pelicans, yel-

The factory near Lake Magadi, in Kenya, where a slurry made from crushed lake-bed deposit and water is kilned to produce soda ash and salt. Nearby wildlife appears to be unaffected.

low-billed storks, and African spoonbills feed at the Lake, and many species breed there, including avocet, pratincole, and three species of sandplovers one of which, the East African race of chestnut-banded sandplover (*Charadrius venustrus*) has few other nesting sites. Other birds visit the area on their migrations, and there are many land birds in the area including the Masai ostrich (*Struthio camelus*) and secretary bird (*Sagittarius serpentarius*) and the pale chanting goshawk (*Melierax poliopterus*).

On the poor pasture around the Lake there are several species of large herbivores. Lions are occasional visitors, as are hyenas, mongooses, honey badgers, and wildcats, and jackals are more common. A leopard was once evicted from the ladies' changing room at the local sports club!

The operation at Lake Magadi was planned without particular consideration for the natural environment but, over the years, it has proved benign. The factory and town, which might cause disturbance, are located out of the way, about 15 kilometres (9 miles) from the area most densely populated by birds. The factory effluent consists

Spirulina grows abundantly in the alkaline lake water and is eaten by large flocks of lesser flamingoes (Phoenicopterus minor) *which are herbivorous.*

only of returning lake water, the gaseous emissions only of carbon dioxide and water vapour, and dust from the factory, which is the same as the soda from the lake, quickly settles nearby and seems to cause no harm.

Oreochromis alcalicus *is the one species of fish that also feeds on the* Spirulina.

the pharmaceutical industry, which is part of the chemical industry. Each year the major companies screen 15 000 or more compounds in the hope of finding a new product.

AN EVER-CHANGING INDUSTRY

This restless enterprise, always adapting, always changing, ever searching for new ideas, new compounds, new products, has contributed perhaps more than any other industry to the standard of living we enjoy. Yet its success imposes a heavy responsibility upon those who work in it to protect the safety and health of all those who may come into contact with the substances it uses, and to protect the plants and animals in the natural environment. In part, this is a process of learning from experience and, when harm is done,

Paraquat, a herbicide used to kill a wide range of grasses and broadleaved weeds, is made at this factory at Madras, India.

steps are taken to make sure the same incident cannot recur. The Minamata incident, in 1959, when villagers were poisoned by eating fish and shellfish contaminated with organic mercury discharged from a chemical factory, led to increased care over the fate of heavy metals. The accident at Seveso, Italy, in 1976, when an accident at a herbicide factory caused the release of dioxin, led to the EEC 'Seveso Directive', regulating the storage and transport of hazardous chemicals; and the accident at a chemical factory at Bhopal, India, in 1984, led to a review of operating procedures in factories installed far from the countries in which they were designed.

SAFETY AND THE ENVIRONMENT

The industry has always done its best to protect its own workers from exposure to chemicals that might harm them, and its

own installations from damage by the materials being processed. Factory owners learned very soon after the industry began that certain of their waste products could be harmful if released into the natural environment and they tried to control emissions, not always successfully, although there was legislation to help, and an inspectorate to police it. In Britain, the Alkali Act, regulating emissions from chemical factories, became law in 1863 and, by the time the first inspectors were appointed, in 1880, their role had been expanded and they were called 'Alkali and Other Works Inspectors'. As the range of

---

Emission control and testing products for their safety are not new ideas ...

---

chemical products has expanded, so it has become necessary to consider the safety of the products themselves when they are used, especially in the case of entirely new compounds that did not exist at all until chemists invented them. Emission control and testing products for their safety are not new ideas but their importance has increased greatly as analytical techniques have advanced.

The research that allows it to observe and manipulate chemical reactions with such subtlety also allows it to detect the presence of compounds in almost vanishingly small concentrations. It is now a matter of routine laboratory analysis to detect the presence of substances in concentrations measured in parts per billion or in some cases even parts per trillion. It is like observing and measuring accurately the presence of one grain of salt in a full swimming pool — and what can be measured in a swimming pool can also be measured in the natural environment, outside the factory site.

Today it would be considered grossly irresponsible for a chemical company to

market a product without first considering the effects it might have on the natural environment, and a large proportion of the research needed to discover those effects is conducted and paid for by the companies themselves. The story of CFCs provides a good illustration.

The chlorofluorocarbons, or 'CFCs', were developed for a range of uses, in foam plastics, as the working fluid in refrigeration and air conditioning equipment, and, of course, as propellants in aerosol cans, because they were much safer than the compounds they replaced. They will not burn like hydrocarbons, will not freeze the skin like carbon dioxide, and are not poisonous like ammonia. The ubiquitous presence of CFCs in the atmosphere was detected in the early 1970s, by James Lovelock, better known these days as the author of the 'Gaia' concept; and a few years later, fears were expressed that they might engage in chemical reactions in the stratosphere from which the effect would be a depletion of the ozone layer. Today their use is being phased out, but it took years of research to discover what actually happens in the stratosphere — it is a difficult region to examine and its chemistry involves hundreds of reactions. A large part of that research was paid for by a number of chemical companies including ICI and Du Pont. The latter first marketed CFCs, under the trade name 'Freon', and the two leading CFC manufacturers, Du Pont and ICI, began work to develop alternative compounds which have little or no ability to react with ozone. Both companies firmly support the 1987 Montreal Protocol on the Ozone Layer.

ENVIRONMENTAL RESEARCH LABORATORY

In 1948, at Brixham, in South Devon, ICI opened a laboratory to test marine paints. It was not long, however, before the Brixham scientists found themselves studying the effects of industrially manu-factured chemicals on aquatic life. Today the Brixham Laboratory is the principal ICI environmental laboratory and it enjoys a worldwide reputation for the quality of its work. The substances whose effects it tests are produced mainly by ICI

> *ICI environmental laboratory ... enjoys a worldwide reputation for the quality of its work.*

but it also undertakes research for other organizations. Essentially, the aim is to discover what happens to a substance when it enters the environment. Does it break down chemically into harmless compounds? Is it dispersed by the water, in soil, or by atmospheric processes, and

ICI's principal environmental laboratory stands beside the harbour at Brixham, a busy fishing port and holiday resort in South Devon.

diluted to harmless concentrations, or does it accumulate somewhere? How does it affect the many different kinds of living organisms that may be exposed to it?

Much of the research is conducted within the Laboratory itself, where natural processes can be accelerated and com-puter models can be built to reproduce under closely monitored conditions what happens when factory wastes mix with sewage and enter a sewage treatment works. It is important to know, for example, whether a particular compound will harm the bacteria responsible for breaking down sewage and so retard the purification process. Detailed measure-ments of the way water moves through a particular river, estuary, or coastal water are used in modelling and provide scien-tists with a good idea of what will happen to substances released at specific places and allow them to find the safest places to site outfalls. Similar studies are applied to the dispersion of substances in soil and air. The biological effects of compounds

Grab sampling from the Brixham Laboratory trawler, in which samples of water from particular places are collected for laboratory analysis.

are measured by observing carefully the health of the most sensitive aquatic organisms when different concentrations are added to the water in which they live.

Work at the laboratory bench is supported by extensive field work. Brixham Laboratory has its own small hovercraft which makes it possible to move quickly and safely across mud flat and sand banks to take samples. Its own trawler is used to take samples of water and measure the direction and strength of currents. Harmless red dye is released into open water to measure the rate at which substances are dispersed and diluted, and divers take samples and make direct observations below the surface.

It is not enough, of course, for the scientists simply to identify the harm a particular activity may cause. Their job is to find answers to environmental questions, but at the same time to provide solutions for industry, so when they say 'You mustn't do this', they can follow it with 'Do that instead'. It makes them innovators. Some years ago a factory was found to be discharging an effluent that

It would be difficult for Brixham Laboratory scientists to take samples from shallow water, soft sand, and mud were it not for the freedom of movement provided by the hovercraft.

contained very small amounts of chloroform, a solvent used in the laboratory. Chloroform is very toxic to bacteria and would have inhibited treatment in the sewage works. The Brixham scientists designed a tower into which sewage is released at the top, air at the bottom, and the flow of air carries away the chloroform. The process is called 'air stripping' and, since it was installed, the sewage works has had no trouble from chloroform.

... Brixham Laboratory is well funded, ...

All research is expensive, and this kind of environmental research is especially so, because it must range so widely. The

The Brixham Laboratory is fully equipped to conduct a wide range of tests to a high standard. Above: Substances are added to water to investigate effects on aquatic organisms. Right: A variety of organisms is employed. In these tanks fish and shellfish are being examined.

Brixham Laboratory is well funded, however. Its analytical equipment is the most modern and its computing power formidable. Its store of information, about hazards associated with particular chemicals, dealing with emergencies, and about environmental legislation throughout the world, grows constantly.

The Laboratory, established by ICI for its own purposes, is now able to serve the community much more widely. It can help when someone needs to know how to plan an industrial operation with the minimum adverse effect on the environment, in any part of the world.

The chemical industry, which has contributed so much to our standard of living and, indeed, to our way of life, was once regarded as a major cause of environmental damage. It was as though harm to the environment was the price we had to pay for our enjoyment of the goods the industry supplied. Traces of that image may linger, but the reality is quite different. Not only are chemical manufacturers highly aware of the damage their operations might cause and have caused in the past, they are also well informed at the most detailed and technical level about the fate of their products once they enter the environment, and are becoming

> *... chemical manufacturers ... are becoming highly skilled at avoiding new damage and removing traces of old damage.*

highly skilled at avoiding new damage and removing traces of old damage.

River Tees

The Tees rises on Cross Fell, in the Pennines, and flows through the Upper Teesdale National Nature Reserve, designated following the botanical survey funded by ICI at the time of the building of the Cow Green Reservoir. It crosses the Whin Sill, possibly the relic of an ancient boundary between two of the Earth's crustal plates, past the waterfalls of Cauldron Snout and High Force — the most powerful waterfall in Britain. By the time it enters the North Sea at Teesmouth it has covered about 150 kilometres (93 miles).

Despite its idyllic origin, the Tees has long been an industrial river. Lead was once mined in its valley, intensively between 1760 and 1870, and it passes close to the coalfields of Durham and the ironstone fields of Cleveland. Stockton-on-Tees and Middlesbrough stand on its banks, and Darlington is situated on the banks of the Skerne, one of its tributaries. The river has been used by the iron and steel, shipbuilding, chemical, and oil industries, and 150 years of industrialization have left scars.

TEES-SIDE NATURE RESERVES

Today it is changing. Factories are steadily reducing the discharges of treated or untreated effluent into the river, so the quality of the water is improving and, little by little, derelict land to either side is being made fit for wildlife. Cowpen Marsh, on the northern bank, is a nature reserve,

Winter at Saltholme Pools Wildlife and Conservation Area, a place of great ornithological value that is within sight of the industrial installations on the banks of the Tees.

leased by ICI in the 1960s to the Royal Society for the Protection of Birds. It is now managed by the Cleveland Wildlife Trust, and a disused quarry near the Billingham fertilizer factory, given to the Trust by ICI, is now an important site for plants, including orchids, and butterflies.

To the south lies ICI Wilton, one of the largest petrochemicals and plastics complexes in Europe, but two-thirds of the Wilton Estate is marsh, woodland, or farmland, rich in wildlife. Cleveland County has appointed an ecologist as warden of 90 hectares (225 acres) of the Estate which ICI has leased to the Council as a reserve, open to the public, for conservation and educational use. Its woodland is among the oldest in the county, with a rich ground flora and an abundance of insects and birds. Elsewhere the company protects and manages valuable sites itself, usually because they are surrounded by industrial installations and there is no public access. The Saltholme Pools Wildlife and Conservation Area is one such site, of ornithological importance, and the saltmarsh habitat is now protected at the North Tees Brinefields. The Brinefields are in continuous use, but of importance for their plants and insects and because they attract many small wading birds, including lapwings, and particularly ringed plovers, which raise young on the gravel roads more successfully than on public beaches where they suffer from disturbance. At other ICI sites there are even roe deer, badgers, and kingfishers.

Birdwatchers attracted by a rare bird that has arrived in an industrial area. These kinds of birdwatchers are sometimes known as 'twitchers'.

COMPANIES IMPROVE HABITATS

Other companies are also improving wildlife habitats on their sites, in collaboration with local authorities and with conservation groups. The success thus far demonstrates that, with proper management and care, modern industry and wildlife can prosper side by side, and that in years to come many older sites may be helped to recover.

Guano

What was perhaps the earliest fertilizer industry began around 1810 in Peru, with the exploitation of guano — a Spanish word derived from the Quechua word *huanu*, meaning 'dung'. Found in Baja California, Africa, and the United States, as well as along the western coast of South America, guano is an accumulation of droppings, food wastes, and the dead bodies of birds, bats, or seals, and it contains up to 16 per cent nitrogen, 12 per cent phosphate, and 3 per cent potash.

On favoured breeding sites, the deposits are sometimes vast. As the value of guano became recognized, its export became economically important to both Peru and Chile. By 1856 Peru was exporting 50 000 tonnes of guano a year from a coast where birds congregate at densities of up to 2 million per square kilometre (5 million per square mile) and eat about 1000 tonnes of fish a day. On the Lobos Islands, off the South American coast, seal guano deposits are 70 metres (230 feet) thick, and caves in Missouri contain around 16 000 tonnes of bat guano. In one cave in the Grand Canyon, there is estimated to be 100 000 tonnes.

GOVERNMENT PROTECTION FOR SEABIRDS

Guano is such a valuable commodity there is a strong incentive to protect its source. The Peruvian Government protects the seabirds along its coast, but the original source of the guano is to be found offshore, where upwellings in the northward-flowing Peru (or Humboldt) Current bring

Collecting guano is an important industry. These guano huts and the loading dock are at Islas Ballestas Paracas, Peru. The Peruvian Government protects the birds that make the guano.

cold water, rich in nutrients, to the surface. The nutrients provide a base for a food chain that sustains one of the world's largest concentrations of fish, and the birds feed on the fish. From time to time, the upwellings cease and the fish disappear, when warm surface water flows eastward across the tropical Pacific in a climatic event known in South America as 'El Ninõ'. There are fears that global warming due to the greenhouse effect may make such events more common, with many possible consequences, one of which is a reduction in the tropical Pacific seabird population, and thus in the production of guano.

Right: *A blue-footed booby with its chick on rocks covered in guano deposits.* Below: *A cliff covered with guano, and the birds that make it, at Islas Ballestas Paracas, Peru.*

CHAPTER 10
TRANSPORT AND COMMUNICATION

There is, so they say, nothing new under the Sun. Had you lived in China about 2500 years ago, during the reign of the Chou dynasty, not only would you have been able to travel that vast country by road, but you might have remarked on the power of the Commissioner for Highways, a government minister. The roads were well made and they were classified, according to the purposes for which they were intended and their width, into five grades. The system was not much different from the one used in most countries today, and the traffic laws were also similar. There were regulations governing the permitted weight for vehicles; there were speed limits; and there were laws to regulate driving in conditions of traffic congestion.

ROMAN ROADS

In Roman times you could have travelled on well-made roads from what is now northern England all the way to the Channel, and from its southern shore all the way to the Euphrates. Remade and upgraded, many modern roads still follow

Still in good condition, this stretch of Roman road is near Aleppo, Syria.

the old Roman routes. In Britain, much of Ermine Street has become the less romantically named A1(M), and cars speed along Watling Street although their drivers may be unaware of the fact. The Via Appia, built in 312 BC as one of the

Roman roads ... popular with ramblers and backpackers, ...

principal routes into Rome, has retained its name. Other Roman roads have become footpaths, popular with ramblers and backpackers, and, in yet other places, remnants of the original road still exist and you can see them. Some 1500 years have passed since Roman workmen last repaired them. The fact that remnants survive shows how well made they were. In fact, they were made in much the same way as modern roads. Layers of sand were covered by slabs of stone set in mortar, covered in turn by concrete made from crushed stone mixed with mortar, and the surface layer was made from gravel and mortar mixed to make a different type of concrete. The roads were cambered, for drainage, and fairly smooth.

The Romans also invented other institutions we may like to think of as essentially modern. Spaced at intervals of about 15 or 20 kilometres (9-12 miles) what we would recognize as service areas provided a range of facilities, and every 50 or 60 kilometres (31-37 miles) accommodation could be obtained in what today we would call motels. There was a postal

Romans also invented ... service areas ...

service, too, with mail being carried along the roads according to regular schedules.

Roads became necessary with the invention not of the wheel but of the war chariot, around 1800 BC. This was fast and light, and proved a devastating weapon when driven by the Hittites who first used it, but it was also delicate. Its light weight was achieved by having only two wheels, with the chariot itself balanced carefully on the axle, and, instead of being solid, each wheel consisted of a rim attached to the axle by spokes. A chariot needed a smooth surface if it was to arrive in one piece at the end of a long journey.

BY RIVER, SEA, AND CANAL

During the long period before roads were built, the most practical forms of transport moved by water. Rivers were used wherever a boat could ply them and, 3000 years ago, the Phoenicians were using sea-going ships for trade. The boats and ships had to be invented and built, but all the 'highways' existed naturally. At

A barge carrying sightseers in a lock on the Kennet and Avon Canal, near Hungerford, Berkshire.

The Suez Canal, providing a short route between Europe and Asia, is always busy. There are plans to widen and deepen it.

made it possible to travel by inland waterway from the Cam at Waterbeach, Cambridgeshire, as far as the Humber and to York, and the Foss Dyke linked the Car Dyke with the River Trent. The canals in Belgium, the Netherlands, France, and Germany are linked together, giving access by water to a large area of northern Europe, and the USSR has some 143 000 kilometres (88 875 miles) of navigable inland waterways carrying hundreds of millions of tonnes of cargo a year.

Although canals may seem old-fashioned to those of us accustomed to fast cars and aeroplanes, they are still important, and the vessels that sail them often

least, they did until people started to construct canals, as artificial waterways. Between 1500 and 1900 the total length of canals in Europe expanded constantly. Canals were a source of much national pride and international competition, but they were not really either a new or a European invention. Pharaoh Sesotris I built what may have been the first canal in the world, in about 1875 bc, to provide a by-pass to the First Cataract on the Nile through which vessels could be towed. His canal was 80 metres (262 feet) long, 11 metres (36 feet) wide, and 8 metres (26 feet) deep. Even the Suez Canal was not the first to link the Mediterranean and Red Seas. Sesostris I started the building of the first one, 30 metres (100 feet) wide and 12 metres (40 feet) deep, between the Nile Delta and the Red Sea. Later conquerors enlarged it, but part of it was blocked for military reasons by the caliph al-Mansur in the eighth century and eventually it filled with silt and was abandoned.

The Chinese built canals, starting in the third century bc, and so did the Romans, in both cases most commonly to link navigable rivers. The Car Dyke in Britain, for example, was a Roman canal that

provide the most economical means for transporting bulky, non-perishable cargoes. This is especially true when the canal leads to the sea and allows seaports to be developed far inland where goods can be loaded and unloaded close to the areas that produce them or where they will be used. The Manchester Ship Canal, opened in 1894, made inland Manchester into an important trading port.

Canals may also link one sea with another. Fees paid by ships passing through the Suez Canal, opened in 1869, earn Egypt some $2 billion a year, and there are plans to widen and deepen it. The Panama Canal, linking the Atlantic and Pacific through a complicated system of locks, was completed in 1914 and about 150 million tonnes of cargo a year are carried through it.

Those great navigational canals, providing short cuts for shipping that formerly had to detour around the Capes of Horn or Good Hope, were joined in 1959 by the St Lawrence Seaway. Although the Erie Canal, completed in 1825, linked New York City to the Great Lakes, this joint United States — Canadian venture is much grander. It allows ocean-going

Miraflores Locks, in the Panama Canal, with a ship in each lane. The Canal has many locks because the waterway between the Atlantic and Pacific crosses high ground inland.

ships to travel up the St Lawrence river, past Montreal, and into Lakes Michigan and Superior, and lake shipping to reach the lower St Lawrence and the sea, a total distance of almost 2200 kilometres (1370 miles) from Montreal to the head of Lake Superior. Most of the ships carry bulk cargoes of iron moving westwards to the industrial regions around Detroit and Chicago, and grain moving eastwards from the prairie farms to the west of Lake Superior. The system of dams and locks includes one power dam with thirty-two generators together capable of producing about 1.8 megawatts of electricity.

Ocean-going ships have little effect on the oceanic environment but they can cause pollution where they travel in large numbers through waters whose volume and movements are not large enough to disperse their discharges. Some years ago the Mediterranean, through which most of the world's tanker fleet sails to and from the Middle Eastern oilfields, suffered serious pollution from ships washing out their tanks at sea. It is now illegal for a ship to clean its tanks in this way, but garbage dumped from ships continued to

Rubbish left by visitors and washed ashore from ships combines to pollute this beach on the Spanish Costa Brava.

pollute inshore waters in many places. Such dumping is now strictly controlled by laws that distinguish categories of waste according to the ease with which they are degraded naturally, and stipulate clearly what may and may not be discharged inside a series of bands at specified distances from the coast.

A canal built to link two seas might appear to link the waters of those seas and to provide a route by which living organisms endemic to one sea might migrate to the other. The ecological consequences of such mixing or migration could be grave but, in practice, it is very unlikely to happen. The canal has to be cut through land that rises above sea level and it would be far too expensive, if it were technically possible at all, to excavate down to sea level along the entire route. Such canals consist of discrete stretches of water, each at its own level, punctuated by locks to raise or lower vessels to the level of the next stretch. There is very little mixing of water between the sea at one end and that at the other, and the locks form a barrier preventing the migration of marine organisms. The construction of an inland canal causes temporary disturbance to habitats but, once work is completed, the canal has no appreciable adverse effect on the natural environment, although its existence encourages industrial development along its banks.

As faster means of transport emerged to challenge their highly profitable virtual monopoly, canals fell into disfavour in Britain, and also in the United States where the government actively encouraged the railway companies to compete against canal owners to reduce transport costs and about half of all canals were abandoned. The United States canals revived later, and those of mainland Europe were little affected by competition from the railways but, in Britain, the decline was not arrested until quite recently, as canals found new friends and new uses. The warehouses and factories

Saltmarshes and mudflats support vast populations of invertebrates which, in turn, provide food for many wildfowl and wading birds. These mudflats are at Pagham Harbour, Sussex.

were demolished or preserved for their historical or architectural merit; the once grimy towpaths are now bordered by flourishing vegetation; the locks are being repaired and the canals dredged, restored, and re-opened for the enjoyment of holidaymakers.

This revival forms part of the growing popularity of watersports and sailing. These bring much enjoyment to many people, but they can also bring ecological damage. Powerboats are much faster and noisier than traditional barges and cause

... once grimy towpaths are now bordered by flourishing vegetation; ...

much more disturbance to wildlife. They also produce large washes that can erode banks, damaging vegetation and the bankside burrows of small mammals. Where large numbers of boats congregate, always in sheltered waters, the wastes they discharge can lead to serious pollution, and some antifouling paints, now withdrawn from use, have poisoned species they were not intended to harm.

Where a natural waterway is 'canalized',

habitats are likely to be damaged. Usually the work involves dredging, deepening, and sometimes widening a channel to give access to shipping, and this may alter the way water flows and consequently the way silt is deposited. Sedimentation is the process that controls estuarine environments. The flocculation of minute particles that occurs when saline tidal water encounters fresh river water causes the particles to settle. This creates mudflats, rich in nutrients, that support vast populations of micro-organisms and small invertebrate animals, and wading birds feed on the invertebrates. Tidal water, flowing over the mudflats and collecting nutrients from them, floods slightly higher ground to either side, creating salt marshes, with plants that can tolerate salt water and their own populations of birds. The estuary of the Tees was once a vast area of mudflats, sandbanks, and salt marsh, most of it lost following the dredging of the deep-water channel in 1852. This began to drain the mudflats and, before long, engineers completed the process. The estuary was reclaimed and factories built on it. The loss was not really the fault of water transport, even so, because the Tees was of much less commercial importance earlier. The change was due to the opening of the first railway, in 1825, which made it possible to bring coal to a previously inaccessible area.

The coming of the railways

Iron-wheeled vehicles were being towed along iron rails in the sixteenth century, but only locally and for short distances. To be really practicable over longer distances, the vehicles needed to be self-propelled, and the invention of the steam-powered locomotive, introduced on the route between Stockton-on-Tees and Darlington in 1825 and between Liverpool and Manchester five years later, revolutionized the entire concept of transport.

With their ability to move large, heavy loads cheaply and quickly, railways made the remotest regions accessible to industry and commerce. This train belongs to the Indian Southern Railway.

The early 'canal mania' was followed by a railway mania in Britain, starting around 1830, and in the United States a few years later, in which many fortunes were made and as many lost. By the time it ended, the interior and west coast of the North American continent had been opened to commerce, the railway network extended into the remotest corners of Europe, and railways were being built in most other parts of the world.

The railways served industry, but, with their demand for steel for building rolling stock and for rails, brick and stone for station buildings and track ballast, timber for sleepers, and coal for fuel, they became an industry in their own right, and stimulated other industries. Despite the present nostalgia for the days of steam power, their effect on the natural environment was less than benign. For more than a century they chuffed and rattled their way through the industrial heartlands, past stations, most with coalyards to keep them fuelled, puffing the ash, steam, and unfiltered smoke that contributed greatly to the fogs and smoke-laden 'pea-soupers' for which London especially was famous but which afflicted most cities. It was a source of pollution that was impossible to control, unlike pollution from stationary engines in factories, and it continued until steam gave way to the much cleaner diesel engines. In the countryside the pollution was less severe but fires were common in nearby vegetation, ignited by sparks emitted by locomotives. Most of the time the sides of railway cuttings were scorched, black deserts, and, where the track ran along embankments, it was not unknown for passing trains to set fire to crops in adjacent fields.

The introduction of diesel engines eliminated the fire hazard and reduced pollution greatly, and electrification brought an end to air pollution. The railways became clean and the trackside vegetation returned, followed by the animals associated with it. There have been some curious results. Oxford ragwort (*Senecio squalidus*), more spreading and bushy than common ragwort but with similar bright yellow flowers, earns its common name because it was first recorded, in 1794, growing on walls in Oxford, having escaped from the Botanic Gardens. The plant comes from southern Italy but it is now spreading rapidly alongside roads and railways in England and Wales, although it is still rare in Scotland and Ireland. Presumably it finds conditions favourable close to the stone of walls and road and rail ballast. It is also

The bright yellow flowers of Oxford ragwort (Senecio squalidus), *growing on a derelict building.*

Disused railway lines

As you travel by train into the centre of any large city, look carefully from the windows at the sides of the track. You may see such plants as the primrose, more typical of woodland clearings and country hedgerows, or heather, carried down from the moors perhaps. Lupins grow beside the tracks around Birmingham, and bladder-senna around London. As diesel and electric engines replaced steam, the sides of railway lines began to develop a rich wildlife just as motorway verges did later. Rabbits have moved along them and there are now rabbits, as well as grey squirrels, in Princes Street Gardens, in the centre of Edinburgh but beside the railway. Foxes, more opportunists than dedicated predators, have moved into the centres of many cities, arriving by rail, though not as passengers.

In many parts of Britain, however, railways have been closed and the tracks removed. Where the land has not been developed for other uses, this has allowed these linear wildlife refuges to develop more fully, but in close association with people because abandoned railway lines can make excellent footpaths and bridleways that soon become very popular.

As you walk along one of these disused tracks, you may see many plants that originally escaped from gardens. Buddleia is widespread, and the common rhododendron has acquired the status of an aggressive weed that has to be controlled. Gorse and

Above: *A crested newt, at home in a ditch.*
Right: *Wild flowers growing along a disused track at Toddington, Gloucestershire.*

bramble will move in and, where the ground does not slope too steeply, trees will follow as the natural succession moves toward mixed woodland. You can expect to see sycamore, which grows almost anywhere, ash, beech, hazel, and oak. If you know where to look you may find orchids and, in the shade of deep, damp, rock-faced cuttings, there will be ferns, some of them possibly rare, such as the attractive maidenhair fern.

Apart from the birds — usually those typical of hedgerows — and insects, you will see less of the animals, but they are there nevertheless. You may find the tracks or, if you are lucky, the footprints, of badgers, and, around dawn or dusk, you may see a fox. There will be field mice, bank voles, shrews, and rabbits burrowing where the embankments are made from

Badgers are among the many animals that have taken advantage of the semi-natural conditions found along disused railway lines.

earth. Ditches beside the track may hold water all year round, providing a habitat for frogs, toads and newts. Slow-worms are fairly common, and, where the climate suits them, adders find railway tracks con- genial places and may be nu- merous. You may catch a glimpse of one, or be hissed at if you walk too close to the vegetation.

These paths now bring pleasure to large numbers of people, and, because trains are not good at climbing steep hills, they are level and easy to walk. Apart from this, their colonization by wildlife gives them considerable educa- tional value.

said that scorpions may be found living in the vicinity of Ongar station, in Essex, presumably descendants of individuals that escaped from a container in which they were being transported.

EXPANDING THE ROAD SYSTEM

While the railway network was being extended to every part of all industrial countries, the road network was also being developed. Vehicles were horse-drawn and emitted no pollution, but, by modern standards, the roads were narrow and poorly surfaced. In wet weather, the mud thrown up by passing wheels coated roadside plants with an opaque layer that clogged stomata and inhibited photosynthesis. The rich and attractive vegetation that lines so many country lanes today developed only when motor vehicles became so numerous that all roads had to be surfaced to meet their needs. When the rain no longer reduced road surfaces to mud, wheels threw up only water, albeit dirty water, which the plants could tolerate. It is mistaken to suppose that the

Below: *Common ink cap* (Coprinus atramentarius) *pushing up the tarmac on the edge of a road.* Below right: *A little soil caught at the edge of a bridge over a road is enough for some plants.*

lanes live on as reminders of a cleaner world that existed a century ago.

Both roads and railways cut swathes through the countryside and the land they occupy is thus denied to other users. A modern motorway requires a wider belt than a two-track railway. This is sometimes used as an argument for preferring

... wild animals become accustomed to the noise ...

railways to roads but the issue is not quite so simple. In sparsely populated regions, especially where land is unsuitable for agriculture, there is little competition for space and so the issue is irrelevant. In more densely populated regions, where the rural environment is highly valued for recreation as well as for agriculture, large roads must be sited very carefully if they are not to be visually intrusive and if noise from them is not to disturb people visiting the countryside in search of tranquillity.

Road vehicles certainly pollute the air and they are noisy, but the pollution apparently has no serious effect on wild-

life, and wild animals become accustomed to the noise and then ignore it. They benefit from the fact that motorways and railway tracks are securely fenced to keep out people. This leaves the roadsides and tracksides undisturbed by humans, and it is trampling that kills plants and disturbance that drives away small animals and birds. In all the heavily industrial areas of the world these places are becoming valuable refuges for many species. The fences exclude most large animals, such as bears and deer — but also sheep and cattle — although not smaller mammals such as foxes and badgers. This necessary restriction is of minor importance, however, and as more safe crossings through culverts are provided to protect the smaller travellers from being run over, the ecological importance of roadsides and tracksides will increase. Meanwhile, some species — especially birds of the crow family — have adapted to traffic; they can feed on the road surface itself and fly out of the way at the last moment as a vehicle approaches.

Wildlife also benefits from the fact that roads and railways form networks, allowing migration from one area to another and avoiding the risk of species being confined in isolated oases where they are extremely vulnerable to local extinction. This is of major importance in major conurbations, such as those in northern England and the Ruhr.

TAKING TO THE AIR

Airfields also cover large areas to which the public are denied access, and the risk of being run over is reduced. Wildlife may thrive on an airfield, but only if it can tolerate such a flat, exposed environment in which flocks of birds are unwelcome, no tall vegetation is allowed to develop, and tunnelling in the vicinity of taxiways and runways is strongly discouraged.

The airlines of the world now carry more than a billion passengers a year but the rapid growth in air transport dates only from about 1950. As civil aircraft have grown larger, faster, and more numerous, living conditions in the vicinity of major airports have deteriorated because of noise. Remedies cannot be wholly satisfactory for irreconcilable demands have to be satisfied. An aircraft cannot be silenced completely, least of all during take-off, and airports cannot be located so far from urban centres as to place them beyond the convenient reach of passengers.

Regulations have been introduced at many airports to restrict or forbid night flying, and the great thrust of modern aircraft engines has made it possible and safe to require pilots to climb very steeply after take-off to move rapidly away from populated areas — the separation being vertical rather than horizontal. Engine manufacturers have contributed by producing quieter engines. The first civil jet aircraft, the De Havilland Comet, was much noisier than, say, a Boeing 747, and carried far fewer passengers. The turboprop De Havilland Dash 7, now used for short-haul internal flights, carrying about fifty passengers, is so quiet, for an aircraft, and can take off and land with such a short run that it is licensed to fly directly into small, city-centre airports.

Whether or not the pollution of the environment is harmful depends partly on the characteristics of the polluting substance and partly on its concentration. Fears that the growth in air transport would lead to a major reduction in air quality have proved unfounded because, although aircraft engines emit exhausts, and sometimes unburned hydrocarbon fuel, they are too few in number and too dispersed to produce much effect. Interestingly, an airliner crossing the Atlantic consumes between 10 and 20 per cent of the amount of fuel per passenger-mile consumed by an ocean-going liner travelling the same route, and the fuel itself is a more highly refined petroleum product and therefore cleaner. While they fly in

Motorway verges

As you drive through the countryside along a British motorway, sooner or later you are almost certain to see a kestrel hovering a few metres above the ground. If your journey is long, kestrels may well become a common sight and you will cease to remark on them.

The kestrels are hunting for food. In their case, this consists of insects and small vertebrate animals such as mice and voles and to either side of the road such food is abundant. You are also likely to see rooks and crows. They have become good judges of the speed of approaching vehicles, feeding on the remains of animals killed on the roadway and dodging to the side at the very last moment.

LINEAR NATURE RESERVES

Motorways are unlike other roads. They are much larger, of course, but they are also built differently. They have wide verges, partly to help isolate the traffic from the surrounding land and partly to control the movement of water in the vicinity of the road. The verges are made from earth and, to stabilize them and improve their appearance, they are seeded with about sixty species of plants. The verges are managed but, apart from those engaged in this task, it is illegal for people to enter them so they suffer little disturbance. It is now nearly twenty years since the first verges were seeded, and, some years ago, ecologists began to notice interesting vegetation establishing itself on them. Today the verges are recognized as valuable areas of natural habitat.

Gorse scrub is a common sight, but limestone is often used in motorway construction, and lime-loving plants, such as bird's-foot trefoil, have been able to colonize verges through areas where the local soil is naturally acid. The vegetation provides food and shelter for many animals, and they can make use of anything. Discarded cans, shreds from old tyres, and such long-lasting rubbish is exploited for nesting, and food scraps thrown from passing cars are quickly eaten. Dead animals are disposed of by scavengers, the crows and rooks dealing with larger species, burying beetles with smaller ones. Kestrels are the most obvious of the predators hunting for mice, voles and the larger insects, but owls may visit the verges at dusk, and foxes and badgers may find ways through the fences.

Motorway verges are turning into long, narrow wildlife sanctuaries, and their value is greatly enhanced by the fact that the roads form a vast network permitting the migration of species over long distances. This is happening not only in Britain but wherever such express routes are bordered by verges from which the public are excluded and where management is sensitive.

Left: *The bank vole* (Clethrionomys glareolus) *is a common resident on roadside verges.*
Right: *Plants becoming established on the cutting made to accommodate the M40.*

Provided there is space to land, aircraft can reach anywhere. A Dakota calls upon Indians in the Brazilian Amazon.

the troposphere, the lower part of the atmosphere, the compounds emitted in engine exhausts are removed very rapidly by natural scavenging mechanisms.

At one time, it was feared that, as aircraft came to fly more frequently in the stratosphere, the region of the atmosphere lying above the troposphere, pollutants might accumulate. There is little exchange of air between the two atmospheric layers and the scavenging mechanisms are less effective. It was suggested that vapour trails, formed by the condensation of water vapour in exhaust fumes, and a common sight in the troposphere, might survive to form stratospheric clouds that would reflect incoming sunlight and so affect the climate. This fear was baseless, because stratospheric air is so dry that liquid water droplets evaporate almost at once and vapour trails rarely form at all. It was feared that nitrogen oxides in exhaust fumes would engage in chemical reactions leading to the depletion of ozone in the ozone layer. This fear also proved groundless but principally because the predicted large fleets of high-flying, supersonic transports were never built. If they have any effect at all, the small amounts of nitrogen oxides released by the few aircraft that fly in the stratosphere at present are believed to enhance ozone formation.

SHIPS OF THE AIR

Should the current interest in airships lead to their development as an important component in air transport, many difficulties might be resolved. Except when it is climbing, an airship does not need to expend energy to overcome gravity, because it is lighter than air. Since its engines are required to provide little more than its horizontal propulsion, it can achieve high efficiencies in terms of the load carried in relation to the power of its engines. Nor does it require runways or taxiways, only mooring masts, for it can climb and descend vertically, like a helicopter but quietly because it uses its engine power only for manoeuvring, not to provide lift. Airships are much slower than conventional aircraft, but they can carry heavy loads from city centre to city centre, an advantage that partly compensates for their lack of speed. They might well have survived much longer than they did during their era of popularity, during the 1920s and '30s, were it not for the catastrophic fires that destroyed several of them. Such fires would not occur today, thanks to developments in the chemical industry that have reduced the cost of helium sufficiently to make it practicable for use as a lifting gas, rather than hydrogen. Hydrogen is inflammable, helium is not.

Since they were first developed in ancient times, transport networks, of roads, canals, railways, and now of airways, have exerted a unifying influence on peoples. They have made long-distance trade possible and have allowed people to visit remote places. Traders have a clear interest in remaining on good terms with one another, and experiencing the way of life of strangers helps people towards the understanding of others that can reduce conflict.

SATELLITE COMMUNICATIONS

Our increased love of travel has been accompanied by great improvements in the speed and efficiency of other forms of communication. *Sputnik I*, the first artificial satellite to enter Earth orbit, was launched in 1957, and the first commercial communications satellite, *Early Bird*, in 1965. Radio and television waves travel in straight lines but satellites, the descen-

dants of *Early Bird*, are now used to receive and relay them. Television programmes can be watched simultaneously by people throughout the world. Satellites also carry the telephone calls that once crossed the oceans along sea-bed cables. We can talk directly to people from whom we are separated by vast oceans but who sound to us as though they were in the next room.

The space communications industry could not exist were it not for the existence of the computers that are needed to perform the intricate calculations involved in designing satellites and positioning them accurately. The computer industry, in its turn, could not exist were it not for the wider electronics industry. These three industries now provide a very significant proportion of all the employment in the major industrial countries.

The manufacture of electronic components involves the use of hazardous chemicals but, provided these are handled

Telecommunications have transformed our lives but overhead cables can be intrusive. These British Telecom engineers are removing one of the poles that carried a line along a skyline above Badgers Holt, Dartmoor. The cable is being placed underground.

Reconnecting the Everglades

The sheet flow of water from the Kissimmee Valley through Lake Okeechobee, then through the swamp lands and sawgrass marshes of the Florida Everglades, is one of the best natural water-filtration systems in the world. For thousands of years, this drainage system delivered clean, fresh water into the mangrove creeks and marshes of Florida Bay and recharged the Biscayne aquifer, which today supplies water to the whole of southern Florida.

In 1926 and 1928, however, there was serious flooding as a result of heavy rains and hurricanes. The United States Corps of Engineers was set to work on a flood-control and drainage scheme, which was completed in 1948. Lake Okeechobee is now completely dyked and its water flow controlled by pumps and spillways. While this has reduced the risk of flooding, however, it has created new difficulties, including the eutrophication of the lake and the depletion of the Biscayne aquifer to the point where the water supply to Miami and southern Flor-

ida is under threat. It has also damaged the Everglades National Park because the water flow to it has become more irregular — sometimes raising levels and flooding nests, and at other times virtually ceasing, so the habitat dries out.

ALLIGATOR ALLEY

Now the delicate balance between the economy and ecology of southern Florida is being restored by co-operation and planning based on extensive field studies.

One of the underpasses that allows Florida panthers to cross the road in safety.

population of the Florida panther (*Felis concolor coryii*, the extreme eastern race of the puma) of which there may now be no more than thirty individuals. The Refuge also contains a wide variety of other species and its management is designed to provide habitat suitable for the panther's main sources of food — white-tailed deer and feral pigs.

ANIMAL UNDERPASSES

Traffic accidents are the main threat to the surviving cats, and fears that still more would be killed when the road was up-graded have led to a unique co-operative undertaking by the State of Florida, the Department of Transportation, and the Fish and Wildlife Service. The new highway has been planned from the very beginning with wildlife conservation, and particularly the fate of the Florida panther, in mind although, of course, the new conservation measures will benefit all the inhabitants of southern Florida — human and nonhuman alike. The project has been linked to a 'Save the Everglades' campaign which, it is hoped, will restore by the year 2000 an ecosystem similar to that of the early 1900s.

A major feature of the new road is the provision of thirty-six underpasses for animals, designed and sited with the welfare of panthers in mind.

Good communications are essential for industry and commerce. The up-grading of the state road, known as 'Alligator Alley', to link the west coast with Miami will do much to satisfy the need for transport but this is a highway development with a difference. Alligator Alley crosses some of the finest wildlife areas in the state. Along its southern edge, the road is bordered by the Fakahatchee Strand State Preserve and the Big Cypress National Preserve, two primeval wilderness areas of great importance. The Fakahatchee covers 81 000 hectares (200 000 acres) and contains more than 475 plant species as well as rare and endangered animals — such as limpkin, wood stork, Eastern indigo snake, and

black bear. There are also large populations of less rare species, such as roseate spoonbill, various egrets and herons, red-shouldered hawk, American alligator, and raccoon. Immediately to the north of Alligator Alley there lies the Florida Panther Wildlife Refuge, created primarily to protect the last remnant

PANTHER CROSSING NEXT 7 MI.

Left: An alligator in the Everglades. *Right:* A sign to warn of panthers that may have missed the underpass.

with care, and wastes disposed of responsibly, modern communications have no adverse effect whatever on the natural environment. Nor do they consume resources that might otherwise become scarce. Satellites are small, for example, yet they replace thousands of miles of submarine cable made from copper. Should it prove practicable to recover the

> *... modern communications have no adverse effect whatever on the natural environment.*

cables their copper could be recycled, and meanwhile no further copper cables are needed. Even the smaller copper cables that carry telephone lines over land are being replaced by optic-fibre cables — made from glass, which in turn is made mainly from sand — not to save copper, but because optic fibres can carry more information more efficiently.

DECREASING DAMAGE

Transport and communications, then, are essential to our way of life and have been for many centuries. In recent years, the changes that have taken place in modes of transport, from steam to diesel to electric trains, and the expansion of air travel, have reduced and often eliminated much of the environmental damage of the past, while our communications are now based on industries that are environmentally benign.

A mobile pontoon laying a 15-kilometre (9-mile) long optical fibre cable on the bed of Ullswater in the Lake District National Park. Once completed, the link will be invisible.

CHAPTER 11
WASTE DISPOSAL

WHAT IS WASTE?

It is very difficult, perhaps impossible, to define the word 'life'. Look it up in a dictionary and you will find it described most commonly in terms of the things living organisms do. This is close to the definition biologists use. All living things do certain things, and one of them is to produce wastes. Waste is the inevitable by-product of the metabolic processes by which organisms provide themselves with energy and the materials they need to construct and to repair their own tissue. So far as trees are concerned, the dead leaves lying on the ground are waste, and,

Litter gets everywhere! These cans have been thrown into a palm tree in Puerto Rico.

so far as many animals are concerned, the skin, fur, or feathers they discard during moulting are waste.

Most animals also produce wastes consisting of materials that were never involved in their bodily processes. An abandoned nest is waste, and so is the used bedding thrown from a badger sett. The molehills that dot fields, marking the mole's chaotically aligned tunnels, are made from material excavated during tunnelling. They are waste. You might almost liken them to industrial waste and, although the scale of these 'mining tips' may seem small to us, they must look large to a beetle or to a mouse.

Humans are no different in this regard. We produce waste, from our bodies and

Waste occurs naturally and is not necessarily ugly. Each autumn, deciduous trees discard their leaves which fall to the ground to form leaf litter. This autumn scene is in Richmond Park, London.

as a result of the things we do. Archaeologists can reconstruct entire ways of life from the rubbish middens left long ago by people of whom we would otherwise know little. The differences between the wastes we produce today and those produced by our remote ancestors derive from the increase in the total amount and the way it is concentrated, and in the composition of the waste. In the natural course of events, the wastes left behind by one organism provide food for others. It is the successive breakdown and synthesis of large, complex organic compounds that constitute the mechanism of nutrient recycling. Wastes, then, are not only an inevitable consequence of life, they are necessary to it.

DISPOSING OF SEWAGE

Human body wastes — sewage — are rich in nitrogen and phosphorus compounds, making them a useful source of plant nutrients, and they have been used as fertilizer throughout most of history. It is unwise to use them in this way without prior treatment to kill parasites that may spread diseases but, for thousands of years, they have been used to grow crops, in many parts of the world, by people who were ignorant of the health hazard and endured the attentions of the parasites.

... wastes left behind by one organism provide food for others.

There are difficulties with disposal on land. Sewage sludge is extremely smelly; it may contain poisons as well as parasites; and the tankers capable of spraying it on to fields are large and heavy, so they can be used only in dry weather for fear of compacting the soil. In 1985 the Severn Trent Water Authority and BKW Sales and Services Ltd received the Pollution Abatement Technology Award for devising a major improvement.

The key to the winning system is an 'umbilical' hose. The tanker, equipped with pumps and powered hose reels, is parked off the field. The sludge is pumped through the hose to a tractor, towing the hose behind it, fitted with a device that injects it 15 to 20 centimetres (6-8 inches) below ground level. The tractor is light enough to work in all weather conditions; the hose is long enough for an 18-hectare (45-acre) field to be treated without moving the tanker, and the sludge can be injected at the rate of 90 000 litres (20 000 gallons) an hour, or about 800 000 litres (176 000 gallons) a day. No sludge appears on the surface so there is no smell and parasites are trapped below ground where they soon die.

Discharged into rivers or coastal waters, sewage promotes plant growth. This increases the amount of food available to animals and the aquatic population prospers. In principle, the discharge of sewage into water may be beneficial, but the amount discharged is critically important and it is easy to overload the system.

Aquatic animals and plants require oxygen for respiration. and they obtain it from oxygen dissolved in the water. Cold, fast-moving water is the most strongly oxygenated but even it contains only

Waste being treated to bring it to a standard suitable for discharge into a river. The violent turbulence mixes the water with air, increasing its concentration of dissolved oxygen.

about 12 milligrams of oxygen for every litre of water. Water that is subjected to less turbulent motion to keep it well mixed and bring it into frequent contact

... *the discharge of sewage into water may be beneficial,* ...

with the air will contain less oxygen, as will warmer water because the solubility of oxygen in water decreases as the water temperature rises. Before the nutrients in the sewage can be made available to plants, the sewage must be decomposed by bacteria, and the bacteria also require oxygen. If the amount of sewage increases, the bacterial population will also increase, more oxygen will be consumed, and plants and animals will be deprived. A river receiving sewage may support little more than the bacterial population for some distance downstream of the outfall, the number and diversity of larger organisms increasing steadily further from the outfall as decomposition nears completion.

Birds congregating around a sewage outfall at Hope's Nose, Torquay. The sewage feeds the aquatic population.

DETERGENTS GO BIODEGRADABLE

The capacity of receiving waters to purify themselves is reduced further if the sewage contains substances that are not easily biodegradable — meaning bacteria have difficulty decomposing them — or that add significantly to the nutrient content. By the early 1960s, synthetic detergents, made mainly from petrochemicals, had virtually displaced soap for washing clothes, but it was found that the detergents themselves decomposed very slowly when the waste water was discharged, causing sometimes spectacular mounds of foam to drift down rivers. The manufacturers identified the cause of the difficulty as the alkyl benzene sulphonate on which most detergents were based. Its molecule comprises a hydrocarbon ring with branched side chains. A compound with an unbranched molecule proved to be readily biodegradable and, in 1964, all the detergent manufacturers changed voluntarily to the new formulation. Since then all domestic detergents marketed in most industrial countries, including the United States and Britain, have been rapidly biodegradable, and the manufacturers, constantly seeking to improve their products, have monitored the fate of the new formulations when they enter the aquatic environment.

Most detergents still contain phosphates, which form complexes with the calcium and magnesium present in hard water and so make the detergent more effective. Phosphates are not removed in the normal treatment of sewage and, being plant nutrients, they can overstimulate plant growth if they enter still or slow-moving water. In modern, 'environment-friendly' detergents, zeolites are used in the place of phosphates. They have a similar effect but are not plant nutrients. The zeolites are a large family of hydrous aluminium silicate minerals that have long been used in water-softening.

INDUSTRIAL WASTE

Industry produces wastes of many kinds and, at one time, much of it found its way into rivers or coastal waters. It was not necessarily poisonous. The processing of china clay, for example, yields a waste composed of water carrying mica and sand, and half of it used to be discharged into local rivers — the Par river in Cornwall became known as the 'White River' and was classified by the water authority as an 'industrial drain'. Since 1968, this waste has been pumped into lagoons contained by dams, the water released into rivers contains less than 100 parts per million of solids, and the 'White River' is white no more.

Where wastes are poisonous, it is necessary to monitor closely the concentration to which organisms are exposed because, for every poison, there is a threshold dose at which it becomes harmful. The World Health Organization assesses the maximum acceptable daily intake for humans of every substance known to be poisonous and sets 'guideline values' at some fraction of this. The EEC accepts these values for most substances and sets them as 'maximum admissable concentrations' that should not be exceeded.

... 'special waste', subject to additional regulations ...

The pollution of soil is treated in a similar fashion but much less is known about the effects of chemical compounds in the soil and so the limits are somewhat arbitrary. They call for constant monitoring and set 'trigger thresholds' at which a soil is considered to be contaminated and the situation should be investigated, and higher contamination levels at which a clean-up operation is required. In Britain, the final disposal of non-hazardous industrial waste takes place under a licence

Flora and fauna on waste tips

You can often tell from far away that you are approaching an urban refuse disposal site because of the large flocks of gulls that have now adopted such places as their own. Opportunist scavengers, they feed on the large quantities of edible food scraps that are to be found and, provided the site has areas free from undue disturbance, the gulls are not alone.

The food scraps that attract the gulls also feed many other small animals, as well as the fungi and bacteria which complete the decomposition of organic wastes, leaving it as humus in which plants can grow. After a time you may find the gulls joined by such opportunist plants as fat hen (*Chenopodium album*), rosebay willowherb (*Chamaenerion angustifolium*), and hoary cress (*Cardaria draba*). These are common enough, but waste tips often acquire the seeds of garden plants which make them something of botanical curiosities. Montbretia may grow on the tip, with asters, Californian poppy, and even the forbidden hemp (*Cannabis sativa*), one of the plants that can germinate from birdseed thrown away with the wastes from the cleaning of birdcages.

HOMES FROM THE SCRAP HEAP

Where there are plants there will be animals, many of them, for which the more durable wastes, such as metal cans, bottles, plastic containers, and scraps of builder's rubble provide shelter and nesting sites — although animals may also be trapped inside containers, or seriously injured by sharp edges or loops of wire. Naturally, there will be mice and probably rats, but there will also be a vast invertebrate population of insects — including butterflies and moths once flowering plants are well established — spiders, slugs and snails, and

A spotted orchid (Dactylorhiza fuchsii) *growing beside the ICI North Tees works.*

earthworms and other inhabitants of the developing soil. Fairly exotic invertebrates may find the tip congenial because the decomposition of organic matter generates warmth. The population of flying insects quite often attracts bats and sometimes lizards and snakes as well.

Industrial waste tips may offer less readily available food, but they, too, become colonized, and, if a tip is large enough, it may eventually come to resemble natural, undisturbed countryside. Grasses stabilize loose material and contribute to the development of soil, which can reach a thickness of several centimetres within five years or even less on a favoured site where plant nutrients are available and where the gradient is not so steep as to erode soil rapidly and make it difficult for plants to anchor themselves. As shrubs begin to appear, the birds will arrive, and they are likely to include species rarely seen in urban surroundings. These 'rural' birds will join and may displace birds more familiar with buildings and gardens. Within a few years, what was once an area of industrial devastation can become a haven for wildlife.

issued by the Secretary of State for the Environment, but waste that could be harmful to human health or might cause serious environmental contamination is classified as 'special waste', subject to additional regulations. These may limit the amounts held in certain places, provide detailed instructions for safe storage or disposal, and, in some cases, may require that the waste be disposed of only under the direct supervision of government officials or agencies appointed for the purpose. Most countries now have regulations along the same lines.

Most countries apply their environmental standards in the form of absolute emission limits but Britain has developed an alternative approach for water, based on environmental quality objectives. This takes account of technical feasibility and also of the likelihood that a pollutant, however inherently poisonous, may actually cause harm. An isolated factory, for example, discharging substances into a large, fast-flowing river or into the ocean well away from the shore causes less environmental damage than a concentration of factories all discharging into the same river or into the inshore waters of an almost land-locked sea. Today the major sources of industrial pollution in the Mediterranean are the rivers that carry wastes into it — although the most serious pollution is caused by untreated sewage.

It is no less important to take account of technical feasibility, for there is little point in imposing standards that cannot be met. Usually a period is allowed before the imposition of new standards to allow technologies to be developed and installed. Such innovation can be pursued with urgency, but improvements cannot be instantaneous. Nor are they necessarily sensible when, as in the case of some pesticide residue limits, the concentration at which action must be taken is below the limit at which the presence of the substance can be detected, or cheap when

the eventual aim is to approach 'zero' limits. Gasoil, for example, typically contains about 0.4 per cent of sulphur by weight and it is proposed to reduce this to below 0.2 per cent. This is feasible but, were it thought desirable to make further reductions, the cost would escalate rapidly, although it is technically possible. In 1983 US dollars, it costs $1900 per tonne of sulphur recovered to reduce the sulphur content to 0.19 per cent, $7000 to reduce it to 0.14 per cent, and $9000 to achieve 0.1 per cent.

DISPOSAL AT SEA

The disposal of industrial wastes at sea, either by incineration in remote areas or by dumping in deep water, sometimes below the thermocline from where water may take centuries to reach the surface

> *... ICI is introducing ammonium sulphate recovery, ...*

layers, is being phased out progressively and, in years to come, all industrial wastes will have to be disposed of on land. At its Billingham plant, for example, ICI is introducing ammonium sulphate recovery, and eventually will recover sulphuric acid as well, so these substances will no longer be disposed of at sea. Safe disposal on land may involve burying it in secure landfill sites above an impermeable layer and beneath either an impermeable surface or up to 2 metres ($6^1/2$ feet) of material arranged in layers through which liquids cannot migrate upwards. Other types of waste require incineration at high temperature in plants designed for the purpose.

SAFE DISPOSAL OF HAZARDOUS WASTES

The technical sophistication required to

Specialized incineration plants can accept waste from many factories and dispose of it under controlled conditions. This is the MAN incinerator unit at the Joliet Plant, in Illinois.

dispose of hazardous wastes safely and in accordance with increasingly stringent regulations has led to the emergence of an industry specializing in waste disposal, and to the transport of wastes from factories to disposal plants. This removes the need for factories to install treatment plant of their own, while restricting disposal to a limited number of installations where the operations can be monitored easily and where staff acquire expertise in dealing with a wide range of materials.

URBAN DUSTBINS

By far the largest volume of waste is not industrial but 'urban'. Urban waste consists of the contents of dustbins from private dwellings, offices where it contains a high proportion of paper, packaging from shops, and food scraps from restau-

rants. Most of it is used for landfill, being dumped in natural hollows and covered with earth. The material is not poisonous but, in recent years, concern has been expressed about the accumulation of methane, produced by the bacterial decomposition of organic matter in the absence of air. Methane production may occur in the airless depths of landfill sites and has been stimulated by the use of plastic containers that decompose rather slowly. If the methane seeps into the air, it disperses quickly and is soon oxidized, eventually to carbon dioxide and water vapour but, when concentrated, it is inflammable. Methane also contributes to the greenhouse effect.

Methane accumulation can be prevented by changing the way the waste is deposited but, in some places, landfill sites have been tapped as sources of methane for use as fuel. There is a garbage-fuelled power station in Melbourne, Australia, and Sierra Leone is planning to import non-toxic household refuse to produce methane for power generation. It is another instance of the use of wastes as raw materials, but others would take recycling much further. The Warmer Campaign promotes the direct use of urban waste as a fuel, burned in incinerators designed to handle it after any reusable materials have been removed from it. In Iceland, for example, a municipal refuse incinerator consumes 10 000 tonnes of industrial and household waste a year and operates a combined heat and power scheme.

RECYCLING

Recycling of waste is both popular and, very often, profitable. One plant in Sydney, that recycles plastics, now has to import acrylic waste to keep its plant supplied, and, at Bayonne, in France, there is a factory that converts 5000 tonnes of plastics a year into stakes. These are used in vineyards, to prevent coastal erosion, and to provide surfaces on which cultured mussels will grow. Metal scrap is commonly recycled, but Alcan Aluminium plans to open a plant in north-west England with a recycling capacity of 50 000 tonnes a year — which is 10 000 tonnes more than the entire British consumption of aluminium cans so, for a time, scrap will have to be imported.

ATMOSPHERIC WASTE

Industrial wastes may also escape into the air but here, too, there have been substantial reductions as health risks have been identified and technologies devised to improve the quality of exhaust gases. Shell, for example, is a major manufacturer of vinyl chloride, the raw material for polyvinyl chloride (PVC). In 1972, its Pernis refinery was releasing vinyl chloride at a rate of 500 kilograms (1100 pounds) an hour. Steps taken to recover more of the vinyl chloride reduced emissions by one-fifth; plant was installed to remove more by steam stripping, adsorption on activated charcoal, and the use of gas traps; and finally a technology was introduced that allowed the reactor to be closed. By 1985, vinyl chloride emissions had been reduced to 4 kilograms (9 pounds) an hour.

The oil industry is very active in seeking ways to reduce the emission of pollutants. The burning of heavy oils releases sulphur dioxide, but total emissions of sulphur dioxide have fallen markedly since 1979 in all the countries of northern Europe, and they are well below the levels of the 1940s. This has been achieved in the case of oil partly by using more low-sulphur crude and partly by removing more sulphur during refining — although this can add considerably to the final cost of the fuel. The use of low-sulphur crudes cannot provide a continuing solution, however, because most of the global reserves of oil have a high sulphur content. As in the case of coal, about 90 per cent of the sulphur in a high-sulphur oil can be recovered using fluidized-bed combustion or flue-gas desulphurization, although both methods leave large amounts of solid waste for disposal.

RECOVERING PETROL VAPOUR

The smell of petrol is familiar at filling stations but the petrol you smell consists of hydrocarbons which pollute the air, and, when you think of the number of fuel tanks that are filled every day in all the filling stations, the total amount of pollution may be large enough to warrant further consideration. Similar pollution also occurs when road tankers are filled and when they deliver their loads to filling stations, and when oil tankers load ballast into tanks that formerly held oil, expelling the residual gases. To combat this source of pollution, oil tankers now have separate ballast tanks and there is talk of installing vapour recovery units at the places where road tankers are filled. Preventing the release of hydrocarbons at filling stations is more difficult. Vapour recovery units might be too expensive, as might be reducing the vapour pressure of the petrol, but it may be feasible to fit vehicles with canisters of an absorbent material.

Litter bins in Mexico City that invite people to separate organic from inorganic waste. This makes disposal much easier.

LEAD-FREE TO LEAN-BURN

Other vehicle emissions are being reduced through the introduction of various technological improvements. More severe processing in the refinery has raised the octane number of petrol to allow the amount of added lead to be reduced and, of course, lower-octane unleaded petrol has been introduced for engines able to use it. Meanwhile, the motor industry has developed catalytic converters that can be fitted to existing cars, provided they use unleaded petrol, and that reduce emissions of unburned hydrocarbons, carbon monoxide, and nitrogen oxides, although they increase fuel consumption — and, therefore, the production of carbon dioxide. It is also developing the 'lean-burn' engine that, with the inclusion of an oxidation catalyst, may achieve equivalent emission reductions, at least for all but the largest cars, without increasing fuel consumption.

WASTE AS A 'RAW MATERIAL'

The generation of waste is the inevitable outcome of any activity, but what is waste to one producer may appear as a raw material and an economic opportunity to another. The chemical industry in particular has always developed by finding as many uses as it can for its incidental by-products and, predictably perhaps, this has led to some of its most exciting innovations and inventions. Recycling is not new but the incentives for recycling have never been greater than they are today, and ways are constantly being sought to convert rubbish into marketable goods. Such is the impetus behind what is now a large industry that, in years to come, its expansion is certain to continue.

This expansion is accompanied by intensive research and development into the consequences of releasing particular substances into the environment and, where they are found to be harmful, of preventing their release. Progress is rapid but improvements cannot be achieved instantly because they may require the invention and installation of novel equipment or the radical modification of long-established industrial processes. We will never reach a position in which no factory ever releases a single molecule of anything at all, for that is unattainable, but there is a more realistic goal. Within the not-too-distant future it should be possible for factories to operate successfully while releasing nothing that is capable of causing serious or lasting injury to human health or to any non-human species.

Oil that has escaped to pollute swamps. This picture was taken in Abu Dhabi in May, 1986.

Human waste used by other creatures

It is a basic ecological principle that, where there is a stock of food, sooner or later something will come along to eat it. Humans throw away considerable quantities of food scraps, and many animals have learned to exploit this resource.

As common as kites

In the Middle Ages, the cities of Europe supported large populations of red kites (*Milvus milvus*). They fed on food scraps and were so common a sight hovering over London that the flying toy was named after them. Today they have disappeared from most cities but black, or pariah kites (*M. migrans*) still feed on waste tips in central and southern Europe and North Africa, and, in India, they are to be found around every bazaar and most homes. In some Indian ports, Brah-

miny kites (*Haliastur indus*) are to be seen sitting on the masts of ships and swooping to pick refuse from the water.

The Egyptian vulture (*Neophron percnopterus*) and hooded vulture (*Necrosyrtes monachus*), both of them small for vultures, up to about 60 centimetres (24 inches) long, are quite indiscriminate about what they will eat. They occur in towns and villages in Africa, and the Egyptian vulture is also found in southern Europe and as far east as India.

Food for mammals

Jackals are also scavengers, and will eat berries and other plant material as well as meat, but they will also kill old and sickly animals. The Indian or oriental jackal (*Canis aureus*)

Below: *A North American black bear (*Ursus americanus*) scavenging from a waste tip.*
Right: *In Canada, a town has been built on a polar bear (*Thalassarctos maritimus*) migration route.*

is fairly common in towns and cities from Arabia to Sri Lanka, and the black-backed jackal (*C. mesomelas*), which is somewhat more fox-like in appearance, occurs in Ethio-

pia and southern Africa. In Europe, the fox (*Vulpes vulpes*), more cautious than the jackal, has found its way into the heart of the largest cities, and their dustbins.

In small towns in the more remote parts of North America, black bears (*Ursus americanus*) have taken to scavenging around waste tips and dustbins. Because these animals can be dangerous, in one gesture of the improved relations between the United States and USSR, a breeding population of 'bear dogs' has been sent from Russia to America. These dogs are bred to scare away bears without attacking them.

Sometimes animals invade towns because the towns are built across their migration routes. In northern Canada, humans have built their homes in the path polar bears take as they move from one feeding ground to another. Bears are creatures of habit, and not to be diverted by the presence of a few houses, but, as they pass through the town, their attention is caught by the pickings to be found in dustbins. Distracted, they pause to eat the food scraps, to the alarm of local inhabitants.

CHAPTER 12
WILDLIFE IN INDUSTRY

Factories occupy land from which the public is excluded, for obvious reasons of safety, and so factory sites are surrounded by fences. Because those who acquire industrial sites must always bear in mind the possibility that the factory will need to expand, or because the industrial operation takes place at points scattered throughout the site, it sometimes happens that, within enclosed industrial land, a substantial portion of the area is not covered by roads or buildings, and humans rarely set foot on it.

MITSUI'S 'DUCK DEPARTMENT'

Where people are kept out, wildlife may move in, sometimes with curious consequences. In Tokyo, one of Japan's largest trading companies, Mitsui, operates from a twenty-five-storey office building and,

outside the building, there is an ornamental pond. In the mid-1980s, a duck arrived at the pond, made a nest, and reared her young, and ducks have used the pond every year since. They spend about a month there, then, as is the way with ducks, the mother and her family of about a dozen ducklings move home, in this case to the moat at the Imperial Palace. The journey to the moat involves the hazardous crossing of a busy street so Mitsui has created a 'Duck Department', with a manager responsible for duck welfare. The ducks are kept under surveillance twenty-four hours a day and, as they prepare to move home, employees stop the traffic to allow them to cross safely. Are the Japanese unusually sentimental about wild birds? Perhaps they are, and

Ducks crossing the road outside the Mitsui offices in Tokyo, on their way to the Imperial Moat.

Above: *Black skimmers* (Rhynchops nigra) *at the Dow Chemical plant. Above right: A black skimmer in flight.*

they are also very tidy people. Because of their architecture, Japanese railway stations provide attractive nesting sites for swallows. The swallows are encouraged but, to make sure passengers suffer no inconvenience, boards are fixed beneath the nests to catch the inevitable droppings.

DOW'S SKIMMER-PARK

Something rather similar to the Mitsui duck story, involving not ducks but black skimmers (*Rhynchops nigra*), happened in Texas, when the Dow Chemical company found itself short of parking space at its Freeport plant and built a new car park for its staff. Skimmers are birds of rivers and coastal waters, and the lower mandible of a skimmer's bill is much longer than the upper. A skimmer feeds by flying over the water with the long, lower mandible below the surface and, when it touches a fish or crustacean, it dips its head to seize the prey. It nests on the ground, on sand, gravel, or shingle. The beaches near the Dow plant are popular with visitors, who disturbed the nesting skimmers. When the company surfaced its new car park with the local gravel, containing a large amount of crushed shells,

the skimmers arrived and made nests among the cars. Eventually, the company decided to abandon the car park to the skimmers. They fenced it, erected notices, and constructed a viewing platform from which the birds could be watched. Although the lack of disturbance suited the birds very well, after a time, plants began

> *... the company decided to abandon the car park to the skimmers.*

to grow through the gravel and, in 1980, the skimmers failed to arrive. Advice was sought from the Texas Parks and Wildlife Service, whose ornithologists explained the preference skimmers have for open beaches with no vegetation. The plants were duly removed, the car park resurfaced with crushed oyster shell, and surprisingly life-like decoy skimmers positioned to attract the birds. In 1981, back the skimmers came and, in 1982 and every year since, several hundred have bred there successfully.

FLORIDA POWER AND LIGHT

These examples may sound extraordinary, but the Florida Power and Light

NASA's Ark

Animals are indifferent to human sophistication. The land around the huge dish antennae at British Telecom's Goonhilly Earth Station in west Cornwall is acid heath, now known for the number of adders that live on it. Goonhilly is a quiet place but, at the Kennedy Space Center in Florida, the noise of a launch is ear-shattering.

The animals ignore the occasional din and seem to

The roar of a shuttle launch from the Kennedy Space Center is of no concern to the inhabitants of the adjacent nature reserve.

have grown accustomed to the large number of visitors. The land managed by NASA, comprising lagoons, marshes, beaches, and inshore waters, is not merely a wildlife refuge, it is a refuge that contains more rare and endangered species than any other refuge on the mainland of the United States. The NASA site adjoins the Merritt Island National Wildlife Refuge, owned by NASA, on whose behalf it is managed by the United States Fish and Wildlife Service.

Many of the alligators in the ponds and canals around the spaceport are 3 metres (10 feet) or more long, and great and snowy egrets fish the pools and marshes, where red-bellied and soft-shelled turtles bask in the sunshine.

GUIDE LIGHTS FOR TURTLES

NASA welcomes visitors, but people are excluded from some areas, for security reasons, and these include stretches of beach that are especially valuable where tourism is an important industry and much of the coast has been extensively developed. The beach is managed by the United States Fish and Wildlife Service on behalf of NASA, and a total of more than 6000 loggerhead and green turtles use the undisturbed stretches to lay their eggs. The loggerhead is classified as 'threatened' but the green turtle is endangered because of the extent to which it has been hunted for its eggs, meat, oil, skin, and shells. Unique among marine turtles, it is herbivorous, feeding on sea grasses. When the

The bobcat (Felis rufus), *a North American species of lynx, thrives on the reserves owned by NASA. It is smaller than the Canadian lynx and less willing to climb trees.*

young hatch, they move immediately towards the sea, guided at night by the difference in light intensity over sea and land. Lights at the spaceport are shaded to the seaward side so the young turtles will not be attracted inland. This measure, combined with the control of predators has increased the survival rate for hatchlings.

BALD EAGLES BY THE ROAD

Visitors are unlikely to see the turtles but they may see bald eagles. For several years a pair

has nested close to one of the main access roads to the spaceport. They ignore the human activity around them and raise their young with great success, unaware of the protection NASA provides for them by means of unobtrusive remote-control television cameras that keep them under constant surveillance.

Bald eagles (Haliaetus leucocephalus) *nest close to a main road, watched constantly by NASA's remote-control television cameras to make sure they are not disturbed.*

Company is one of a number of companies in the southern United States that has alligators in its cooling system. This is a large pond beside the Martin Power Plant. The alligators share the pond with coots, grebes, and ring-necked ducks and, when visitors have seen them, they can move on to the adjacent Barley Barber Swamp reserve, which the Company also owns, and observe its wildlife from a

... alligators in its cooling system.

boardwalk that meanders through the reserve without disturbing it. The company bought the Barley Barber Swamp — named after a former local resident about whom little is known — in 1972 and declared it a reserve when they realized it was a relic of the original ecosystem of the region, partly bald cypress swamp and partly pine forest. The cypresses are parasitized by strangler figs, festooned with Spanish moss — an epiphytic bromeliad (an 'air plant', closely related to those you can buy as house plants) and not a moss — and, in the drier ground, there

One of the cooling lakes outside the Martin Power Plant, used by alligators and many birds.

An anole lizard (Anolis sp), the New World equivalent of the chamaeleon, but more skilled at changing colour.

are palms and palmettos forming a community sustained by seasonal fires caused by lightning. Wild coffee grows there, and cabbage palms and pond apples, with countless ferns, some of them rare. Red-tailed hawks, red-bellied and piliated woodpeckers, turkey vultures, and great horned owls are among the many birds, and the mammals include nine-banded armadillos and bobcats.

INDUSTRY AND WILDLIFE AT TEESMOUTH

Given more space, even the most heavily industrialized region may support a large wildlife population. The lower reaches and estuary of the River Tees, in north-east England, is just such an area. The water used to be severely polluted, with a biochemical oxygen demand (BOD) of

402 tonnes a day in 1970. Since then, however, ICI and other companies have improved the quality of their effluent and, by 1980, the BOD had fallen to about 122 tonnes, and salmon and sea trout had returned to the river. In 1984, ICI contributed to the cost of publishing the results of a survey, conducted by the company's ecology officer, of its wildfowl population. Despite the fact that about three-quarters of the tidal mudflats had been reclaimed since 1960, and despite the great increase in industrial development at Teesmouth, the numbers of wildfowl were found to be much larger than they had been twenty or thirty years earlier. Parallel studies by scientists from

---

... ducks ... frequent the ponds adjacent to the ICI North Tees Works, ...

---

the University of Durham showed that large numbers of wading birds were also thriving on the Tees mudflats. Waders feed on the invertebrates living in the mud. Between one and two million polychaete and oligochaete worms were found per square metre of mud surface, and *Hydrobia ulvae*, a small gastropod, at densities of tens of thousands per square metre. The wildfowl survey recorded sixteen species of ducks occurring regularly at Teesmouth, with a further five that were uncommon or rare visitors. All three British species of swans are found in most years, and, although geese are generally uncommon at Teesmouth seven species have been recorded. Many of the ducks feed on the intertidal mudflats of Seal Sands, but they also frequent the ponds adjacent to the ICI North Tees Works, which comprise the company's wildlife and conservation area of Saltholme Pools and Cowpen Marsh. The marsh is owned by ICI and leased to the Cleveland Wildlife Trust as a nature reserve.

The habitat has long been of international importance for its populations of particular species of birds. There used to be a great deal of wildfowling, much of it illegal, by people shooting from the sea wall bordering the mudflats. Since 1963, this has been greatly reduced by the collaborative efforts of local authorities, wildfowling clubs, the police, birdwatchers, and industrial security patrols.

HUMBER, MERSEY, AND SOLWAY FIRTH

The Humber estuary, to the south of the Tees, is only a little less industrial, with about 10 kilometres (6 miles) of dockside at Hull, on the northern shore, and Immingham Dock and Grimsby on the southern. It, too, supports habitats of several distinct types. Tioxide UK Limited has produced an educational pack listing five nature reserves of particular interest along the estuary. One of them, at Spurn Head, is famous for its waders and wildfowl, but the estuary also has reserves based on reed beds and dune systems, one of which has a population of the rare natterjack toad. Natterjacks have been helped by industry in several parts of Britain. They are found on an ICI plant near the Solway Firth, and on a nature reserve in Cumbria owned by British Nuclear Fuels.

The Mersey is still seriously polluted but there are natterjacks beside the Mersey, too, where ICI, Shell, and other companies have achieved considerable environmental improvements. When leaking oil from a fractured oil pipe polluted the river in 1989, it was the contrast with the relatively clean conditions that made the incident a matter of national concern. Shell, the owners of the pipeline, have cleaned up the spilled oil, and the Shell refinery at Stanlow is a wildlife haven. Rabbits feed on the grass, and foxes and stoats hunt them. Squirrels live in the trees, many species of ducks feed and rest by the waterside, and waders sometimes use part of the refinery site as an extension

Roe deer (Capreolus capreolus) *have been found on ICI industrial sites in Britain and West Germany.*

of the adjacent low-lying fields. Kestrels search for insects and small mammals and, one year, eighteen species of birds nested in a 1-hectare (2.5-acre) strip of woodland, planted to screen one of the tank farms. In addition, the miles of intricate outdoor pipework provide almost limitless space for birds to roost and nest.

INDUSTRY AND LEISURE

Such improvements are of obvious importance for wildlife conservation but, where the public can have unrestricted access to reserves and areas set aside for amenity use, there are further benefits that are no less valuable. Crowded Britain is short of recreational space, and relaxing informally in a rural setting is by far the most popular pastime which is increasing every year. It is so popular that the national parks of England and Wales are at risk of serious damage from over-use, victims, perhaps, of their own success. The Lake District, Peak District, and Dartmoor, in particular, are suffering so badly from erosion, caused by the trampling of too many feet, and severe traffic congestion on fine weekends, that there is talk of rationing public access. If industry can convert former industrial land into country parks and beauty spots close to centres of population they will relieve these pressures on the national parks while, at the same time, providing attractive surroundings that local residents can reach much more quickly and easily.

When an industrial site is developed, anywhere in the world, some species will remain because they can tolerate the disturbance or even benefit from it. They will be common species, such as tough grasses that thrive on cleared land and shade out competitors, and such birds as starlings, which exchange their lost roosting sites in trees for new ones in the eaves of factory buildings. Other plant species, such as birch in northern countries, may benefit because they are early colonizers in a natural plant succession. They cannot tolerate shading but their seeds germinate on ground exposed to direct sunshine, and they grow well until larger trees arrive to shade them again.

Where woodland was cleared to make the site, the habitat may come to resemble a woodland clearing or edge, with a ground flora containing many of the locally natural woodland herbs — the plants we know as the wild flowers of the spring and summer — and the animals associated with them.

If the site is planned well and managed not too zealously,with banks and trees for screening and a variety of planted shrubs, the natural species diversity will soon increase. In Europe, for example, voles and other small mammals will burrow into the banks, warblers, mistle thrushes, pied wagtails, house martins, finches, and robins will claim the roofs of the buildings as well as the trees and bushes, and the insects will include butterflies and bees. In other parts of the world the species may differ, but colonization will occur in much the same way.

Reducing erosion at Golden Cap, Dorset, a popular beauty spot. At 190 metres (626 feet) this is the highest point on the English south coast and the South West Coast Path crosses it.

HABITATS PREVENT POLLUTION

Measures taken to prevent the pollution of nearby water can themselves provide valuable habitat. Reeds (*Phragmites* species), for example, are sometimes planted because they take up plant nutrients, and thus lower the biochemical oxygen demand of discharged water before it reaches a river or the sea. ICI plans to use a reedbed treatment system on Teesside. The reeds themselves could provide raw material for local craft industries, such as thatching, and they can also provide shelter and nesting sites for birds.

Some West German factories, such as the Windel textile plant at Windelsbleiche, use reedbeds in this way, and reeds, together with an area of willow carr, occur naturally beside two ICI plants at Wilhelmshaven. These factories make vinyl chloride monomer (VCM) and, from it, PVC. They both achieve very high environmental standards, and the Atlantik plant, is said to be one of the

Strictly for the birds

The peregrine falcon (*Falco peregrinus*) occurs throughout the world. Although its numbers fell when the accumulation of organochlorine insecticides in its tissues impaired its ability to hatch and rear young successfully, it is now recovering where the use of organochlorines is restricted. It is a bird of the high cliffs, a predator of other birds that catches its prey in flight. When it dives, a peregrine is one of the fastest birds in the world.

Nest sites for birds of prey

The peregrine needs high perches from which it can

Kestrel chicks (Falco tinnunculus) *in an industrial building — a nest site unwittingly provided by humans. Soon they will be hunting for themselves, perhaps along roadside verges.*

watch for prey, and cliffs with narrow ledges where it can nest securely. Its breeding sites are limited because, although there are suitable cliffs along many coasts — and peregrines feed on seabirds — they are much less common inland. Where industrial activity has created artificial cliffs, peregrines may nest provided they are not disturbed during the month required to incubate the eggs and for five or six weeks afterwards, until the young are fully fledged. There have been peregrine nests, for example, very high on the side of the slate quarries at Blaenau Ffestiniog in Wales, directly above the town car park.

Kestrels are less demanding and they, too, are found throughout the world, although the Old World spe-

cies (*Falco tinnunculus*) is not the same as the American (*F. sparverius*) which is also known as the sparrowhawk. Both kestrels will nest in high trees, sometimes in the abandoned nests of crows, on cliffs, or in buildings — the American species nests in holes and cavities, the Old World species in an open nest — and they feed on small rodents, amphibians, reptiles, or insects. This adaptability makes them by far the commonest of all birds of prey and they take full advantage of the high perches provided by humans. They are often to be seen hovering, or sitting on telegraph poles or wires and, although they are less visible on the ledges and roofs of industrial and commercial buildings, they use those perches, too, apparently quite indifferent to the proximity of people — from whom they can easily escape if they wish.

Closer to home — pigeons and starlings

Not all the birds that make use of industrial buildings are so popular. Feral pigeons have become nuisances in cities. They roost and nest on high buildings, feed on scraps, and thrive because their fiercest natural predator, the peregrine, seldom visits their urban homes. Descended

Above: *A nesting box for American kestrels (Falco sparverius) being fixed to the side of a building in Idaho.* Right: *Feral pigeons at roost on the side of an urban building. These birds are regarded as a nuisance, but they consume large amounts of the food scraps we drop carelessly wherever we go.*

from escaped domestic pigeons (pigeons have been domesticated for at least 5000 years), they inherit their habits from their ancestor, the rock dove (*Columba livia*), which nests on coastal cliffs. The starling (*Sturnus vulgaris*) also uses high buildings, but only to roost, not to nest, so it is a seasonal visitor to urban and industrial areas, arriving after it has raised its young.

cleanest factories in Europe. Marsh harriers and buzzards nest on the site, bitterns are known to be present — their call is unmistakable — and muskrats and roe deer are among the mammals that visit. Indeed, the site is well on its way to qualifying as a nature reserve.

On its site at Mandan, in North Dakota, the Amoco Oil Company really has established a wetland reserve, primarily to purify waste water. There are deep pools, marshes, muddy shores, and almost 8 hectares (20 acres) are devoted exclusively to growing maize, wheat, sunflowers, and millet specifically to feed the birds; there are also fields growing alfalfa to produce hay once the wildfowl have finished using the crop for nesting cover. Some of the larger ponds have islands, built by Amoco to provide nesting sites, and more than forty different species have used them. Altogether, 185 species of birds have been recorded on the reserve, including Canada geese (*Branta canadensis*) and American avocets (*Recurvirostra americana*), both of which have bred there. At 'Elk Ridge' Amoco also runs a project to conserve American elk or wapiti. [The European elk (*Alces alces*) is now better known by its North American name of 'moose'.]

British Sugar Corporation established a nature reserve for aquatic birds, ...

Some years ago the British Sugar Corporation established a nature reserve for aquatic birds, at its Allscott sugar-beet factory near Shrewsbury. The processing of sugar beet uses a large amount of water which is allowed to settle before it can be returned to the river. There are fourteen artificial ponds into which waste water is pumped during the processing season, from about October to February, and the water is released into the river in spring. The high water levels in winter attract

wildfowl, the lower levels in spring expose mud that attracts waders, and some of the ponds have been colonized by reed mace and common reed. It is one of the ponds that has been declared a nature reserve to protect about thirty pairs of reed warblers (*Acrocephalus scirpaceus*).

BRINE POND WILDLIFE

Brine ponds attract different species, of fish as well as birds. The Dow plant that has skimmers in its car park also made another improvement. In collaboration with Texas Parks and Wildlife and the Gulf Coast Conservation Association, they installed new brine ponds, which would have made the older ponds obsolete had a use not been found for them hatching redfish (*Sciaenops ocellatus*), a species of drum (also known as channel bass), which are perch-like, carnivorous game fish, and raising them to fingerling size before releasing them into the sea.

Perhaps the birds that have benefited most from the provision of brine ponds are the avocet and the flamingo. The Camargue is an area of about 750 square kilometres (290 square miles) in the delta of the River Rhône in south-western France. Natural salt-water lagoons and marshes fill during the winter and partially dry out during the summer, and the less saline of the artificial lagoons, used to produce some 800 000 tonnes of salt a year by solar evaporation, are virtually indistinguishable from them. The lagoons do not support many species of invertebrates, but those that can thrive do so in vast numbers, providing food for large numbers of wading birds during their spring and autumn migrations. Avocets (*Recurvirostra avosetta*) breed there, along with black-winged stilts (*Himantopus himantopus*), and greater flamingoes (*Phoenicopterus ruber*) breed on islands, some of which have been made for the purpose, forming the largest colony of these birds in Europe. Parts of the

Harvesting salt in the Camargue, where the salt-water lagoons attract large numbers of wading birds.

Camargue are now used to grow vines and rice. This has reduced the area of habitat for the brine-lagoon birds but has attracted other species.

Flamingoes, of the same species but the Caribbean race which are a brighter pink colour, also nest on the salt fields of the Antilles International Salt Company, on the island of Bonaire, in the Netherlands Antilles off the coast of Venezuela, where the company made a reserve specially for them. The reserve was planned in collaboration with several international conservation organizations before salt extraction began because of fears that the operation would damage habitats. Some scientists claim that the change in salinity caused by the saltworks has considerably reduced the numbers of brine flies and to some extent of brine shrimps — which are the principal food of the flamingoes. This is said to have forced the birds to make regular food migrations to the Venezuelan coastal marshes. The company, however, maintains that the migrations are traditional and point out that the poten-

tial feeding area has been increased greatly by deliberate flooding with sea water. The flamingoes continue to breed successfully.

Flamingoes do not occur in the wild in Australia, but, on the Dry Creek Saltfields, on the shores of the Gulf St Vincent, near Adelaide, there are Australian pelicans *(Pelecanus conspicillatus)*, royal (or black-billed) spoonbills *(Platalea regia)*, little egrets *(Egretta garzetta)*, red-necked stints *(Calidris ruficollis)*, and banded stilts *(Cladorhynchus leucocephalus)* as well as black-winged stilts *(Himantopus himantopus)* and many other species. The birds are present in such large numbers that the saltfields were declared a reserve in 1930, soon after work at the site began, and its importance as a bird sanctuary is recognized by the South Australia Government. Some of the lakes were once used by ICI to culture oysters, and, nearby, a lake used to supply the oyster hatchery contains freshly pumped sea water and has a very large fish

Urban fox

In 1979, Oxford University zoologist David Macdonald was telephoned by a factory manager worried because a family of foxes had taken up residence in his warehouse. The workers were far from worried, for they had adopted the fox as a mascot. They left food for it and it would play with them, chasing paper balls until, late every night, it set out to explore the Cowley car factory.

The common red fox is an opportunist. Its natural diet is varied and includes berries and other plant material, for the fox has a sweet tooth, and it will feed on scraps left by humans. It has now moved into most urban areas, al-

Dr David Macdonald is one of Britain's leading authorities on foxes.

though many 'urban' foxes move between countryside and town, and industrial sites offer many corners where it can shelter, earth in which it can burrow, and its keen nose finds plenty of food. Foxes have been seen around many factories — several pairs live on the ICI Wilton Estate, in Teesside — and have often been photographed, for example, in the grounds of the Shell Stanlow oil refinery.

Foxes are attractive animals and usually popular — except with people who keep chickens. They compete with cats for food, but relations are generally peaceful, a cat and a fox sometimes feeding side by side, and should there be a contest with an adult cat, the cat almost always wins, although a kitten may not fare so well. If they are not persecuted, they can become almost tame with humans. At the ICI North Tees Works, one fox that has been known to take food from the hands of its human friends.

SHARING A HOME

Badgers often share their setts with foxes and, where foxes are known to inhabit an area that also has good plant cover and well-drained earth banks, it is worth looking for evidence of badgers, even on an industrial site. There are badger setts on the ICI Wilton Estate, for example, and some have become very tame.

The area in which a fox searches for food — its range — varies widely according to the resources available but, around industrial sites, where resources are often plentiful, it is small, commonly about 90 hectares (225 acres) or even less. A site smaller than this may lie inside a fox range, so the fox will visit it, and one larger may contain part of two or more ranges. Sometimes two foxes will share a range but most ranges are occupied by only one adult and are probably defended.

Right: A fox will usually ignore an adult cat but should there be a confrontation the cat will probably win. Below: 'Basil' and 'Snipes' play-fighting. Fox cubs are very playful and a yard makes a perfectly good playground.

population. The fish have attracted more birds, including the sacred kingfisher (*Halcyon sancta*).

CONSERVATIONISTS IN INDUSTRY

People who work in industry are as likely as anyone else to be wildlife conservationists, with a keen interest in the species they can see close to where they work. High fences exclude the public and this allows parts of the site away from roads and buildings to develop as semi-natural habitat and to attract many species. Nowadays the value of such habitat is recognized and many companies, no doubt spurred on by their own conservationists, do their best to protect their local wildlife and then to disseminate information about it. ICI, Shell, Phillips Petroleum, Gulf Oil, and Conoco are among the large industrial companies that have published books and booklets about the wildlife on or near their sites, and many provide study facilities. The Hartlepool nuclear power station in north-east England, for example, is bounded on three sides by sites of special scientific interest and, in 1970, the Teesmouth Field Studies Centre opened there, with facilities provided by the Central Electricity Generating Board. Since it opened, the building has been enlarged and provided with laboratory equipment and a reference library, and a full-time warden has been appointed.

There are now countless examples of co-operation between industrial companies and conservation groups. Such co-operation can be very fruitful, especially when consultation begins while the industrial operation is still being planned. Industry is often able to provide protected sites that, with advice from skilled conservationists, can be used and adapted to provide rich and valuable areas of habitat and, sometimes, a refuge for endangered species.

Sunset over a rice paddy in the Camargue, France. The temporary ponds attract aquatic birds.

CHAPTER 13
INDUSTRY AND RARE SPECIES

The relationship between industry and the natural environment is often subtle. Obviously, when a factory is built, a certain amount of land is covered by buildings and roads, so it may seem that an industrial development is injurious to wildlife, at least in the immediate vicinity. The impression is misleading. It arises because the obvious fact that no plants can grow on land that is covered in concrete suggests to us that a similar restriction applies to the areas that form part of the site but where there are no buildings. At the same time, we too readily associate factories with essentially urban surroundings which we assume wildlife cannot tolerate. This is to make a distinction that means nothing to other species. A bird seeking a place to roost or to nest will use the wall or roof of a building as readily as a cliff, and will find a telegraph wire no less convenient than a twig. A crevice in a wall will serve many species as well as a hole in an earth bank. Plants require sunlight, water, and nutrients and will grow wherever these occur

... the presence of industry may benefit wildlife, and often does.

provided only that some mechanism exists to transport their seeds to favourable locations.

INDUSTRY SAVING THE ELEPHANT

Many industrial sites support a rich diversity of flora and fauna, sometimes even ranking as nature reserves, and their conservation value often derives from the presence of industry, because this requires land to be enclosed without being put to direct commercial use. So the presence of industry may benefit wildlife, and often does. Other relationships, however, are much less obvious. Industrial products shape our way of life, altering our behaviour and our attitudes to the world around us, and these very fundamental modifications also have implications for

When a building falls into ruin, it is not long before plants take root in crevices between its stones.

African elephants (Loxodonta africana) *that have been wallowing in red mud. They are threatened by illegal ivory poaching.*

wildlife. Consider the case of the African elephant.

This majestic animal has earned a special place in the affections of conservationists, for its fate exemplifies the consequences of human greed. Elephant tusks provide ivory which commands a high price as a raw material for ornaments and, despite vigorous attempts to curb the ivory trade, illegal killing continues. The poachers select the animals with the largest tusks, try to kill as many elephants as they can, and, because their activities are criminal, poachers are often violent, disruptive people who cause much disturbance to otherwise peaceful communities. In 1970 there were estimated to be about 30 000 elephants in Uganda. By 1980, the number had decreased to about 2000, due mainly to poaching but partly to the civil war. In 1976 alone, 200 tonnes of ivory were exported from the Central

African Republic. Obtaining this amount of ivory meant killing between 10 000 and 20 000 elephants. Although there are still believed to be at least a million elephants in Africa, and poaching has decreased, elephant numbers are probably falling. Both African and Indian elephants suffer from loss of habitat, but the Indian species is not threatened by hunting. The tusks of the Indian male elephant are usually too small — the females of this species lack tusks — and the elephant itself is more valuable for the labour it contributes to local economies.

The very word 'Africa' conjures for many of us an image of elephant herds on their long, ponderous migrations, trunks intermittently reaching out to satisfy a prodigious appetite by demolishing a hectare or two of the countryside. The picture is about as far removed as it could be from the one we see when the word 'factory' is mentioned. No one can blame industry for the damage inflicted by the ivory poachers, but neither can most of us suggest any practical way in which industry might contribute usefully to elephant conservation. Yet it was an industrial development many years ago that today allows us to oppose so confidently the killing of elephants for commercial profit.

... industrial development ... allows us to oppose ... the killing of elephants ...

It began with a game and two brothers who were inventors. The inventors were real, and real inventors, unlike most fictional inventors, spend more of their time searching for substitutes for existing products than in devising ways to accomplish things no one has ever dreamed of doing. The game was billiards. Together with its variants, pool and snooker, billiards is played by countless thousands of people all over the world, and in one version or another it has been played for so long that its origins are lost in historical obscurity. Certainly it was popular in the sixteenth century. Edmund Spenser mentioned it and Mary Queen of Scots is said to have complained when her billiard table was taken from her at the time of her arrest, in 1576. Shakespeare mentions the game a little later and it was highly fashionable by the end of the seventeenth century.

The game is played with balls, their number ranging in the modern versions from three in billiards to sixteen in pool and twenty-two in snooker. Because the game calls for a high degree of skill, it is extremely important that the balls are all

of equal size and weight and that they are as nearly spherical as possible so they will roll predictably. They must also be hard enough to withstand repeated collisions without becoming dented or chipped. Traditionally, billiard balls were made from ivory, seasoned slowly and then shaped laboriously. It was the best material available but it was far from perfect because, eventually, an ivory ball loses its shape, and the physical properties of ivory are affected by changes in temperature and humidity.

The inventors were a young American printer, John Wesley Hyatt, and his brother Isaiah. In 1863, a company called Phelan and Collander, which made ivory billiard balls, offered a prize of $10 000 to anyone who could improve on the natural material. John Hyatt dissolved nitrocellulose in ether and ethyl alcohol under pressure and, in 1868, he found that, when camphor was added to this mixture, it yielded a substance that became soft enough to mould in a hydraulic press when it was warmed, whereas when it cooled, it became hard and strong. He and Isaiah took out patents on this substitute for ivory. In fact, they had

Until industry found a better substitute, snooker balls were made from ivory. This room is at Eastwell Manor, in Ashford, Kent.

made the first thermoplastic, and so founded the plastics industry. They went on to invent celluloid, used to make blanks for dental plates, collars, but also combs, ornamental handles for brushes, spectacle frames and other items that until then had often been made from ivory or tortoiseshell. An alternative for one use can be adapted for other uses. Piano keys, for example, were traditionally also made from ivory, but the development of plastics meant ivory was no longer needed.

Since 1920, billiard balls have been made from a phenolic resin, which wears better than the original Hyatt plastic and can be coloured more brightly, but it was the Hyatt invention that proved beyond doubt — more than a century ago — that industry is capable not merely of finding alternatives to natural products we might wish to conserve, but that those alternatives are often superior to the original because they can be designed precisely for the purpose they are to serve. An expert can distinguish ivory from its substitutes by its grain and the fact that it yellows with age but, if these qualities are required, today industry can supply them. This is why we are able to assert that we no longer need natural ivory, that it has no essential use, and that the survival and proper management of the elephant herds are worth far more to us than a raw material industry has rendered obsolete and to supply which magnificent animals must lay down their lives.

IN PLACE OF THE ANIMALS

The case of the African elephant may seem exceptional, but it is not. Whales, once hunted to supply essential raw materials, are still hunted to supply products for which perfectly satisfactory substitutes now exist. The arguments concerning whaling may turn on its possible effects on the breeding viability of whale populations, or on the implications for local economies, but it is no

Industry has found alternatives for all sperm whale (Physeter catodon) *products. These whales are off the California coast.*

The interior of Westerham ragstone mine, where bats roost by day and hibernate during the winter.

longer possible to maintain that whale products themselves are necessary. Many people oppose the killing of animals for their skins or fur, and they can afford to do so because we no longer need to use skins or furs. Garments made from synthetic fibres are warmer and more waterproof, and imitation furs are used to make fashionable garments at least as attractive as those made from real fur.

It is not only materials for which substitutes have been found. Farm tractors and motor cars replaced horses. In 1910, there were about 1.1 million working horses on British farms, and about half-a-million horses were kept on farms for riding or for drawing vehicles. About 650 000 hectares (1 606 000 acres) of land was required just to feed them all. Draught horses have now virtually disappeared and the number of horses kept for riding has been more than halved, releasing land for other uses — which can include public amenity or wildlife conservation if that is what we choose.

INDUSTRY ABANDONS AND RARE SPECIES GAIN

Even dereliction can bring advantages to wildlife, and abandoned land, useless for most purposes, can provide habitat sometimes for rare or endangered species. In Cornwall, where centuries of mineral mining have created more than 4500 hectares (11 120 acres) of derelict land — about 1.25 per cent of the total land area — the generally poor vegetation that has colonized rough terrain where concentrations of metals approach toxic levels provides shelter for some unusual animals. *Araneus adiantus*, for example, is a rare spider that occurs there, and another, the six-eyed *Segestria bavarica*, lives in cracks in the walls of ruined mine buildings. Pipistrelle and greater horseshoe bats roost in mine shafts.

SPECIAL PROTECTION

There are occasions when rare or endangered species are discovered on existing or proposed industrial sites, and special measures must be taken to protect them. Sometimes, the requirements of industry are incompatible with those of conservation and a difficult decision has to be made between one or the other, perhaps with no possibility of compromise. In caves on Mount Etna, Queensland, for example, there are colonies of Australian ghost bats (*Macroderma gigas*) and little bent-winged bats (*Miniopterus australis*) whose survival was threatened in the 1980s because of quarrying by the Queensland Cement Company. For twenty years, conservationists had been urging that the area be designated a national park, and protesters occupied the caves to obstruct the company. In 1988, the Government of Thailand abandoned plans to build the Nam Choan Dam because the reservoir would have flooded the Thung Yai Wildlife Sanctuary which contains several rare mammals, as well as green peafowl (*Pavo muticus)* and white-winged wood ducks (*Cairina scutulata*). The ducks are almost extinct.

Happily, there are many other sites and activities where no conflict occurs. The

White-winged wood ducks at the Slimbridge Wildfowl Sanctuary, close to the heavily industrialized Severn Estuary.

Conoco Oil Company owns land near Galveston Bay, Texas, where it hopes to develop a sanctuary for Attwarter's prairie chickens, birds belonging to the grouse family that were once common on the prairies from Texas to Manitoba but have become increasingly rare as the long prairie grasses that afford them food and shelter have been cleared to grow cereals. Unless active measures are taken to protect them, prairie chickens may become extinct. On the Aransas reserve in Texas, Conoco are also helping in the conservation of whooping cranes *(Grus americana)* which face the very real possibility of extinction. Whooping cranes, which overwinter on the reserve, are the tallest of all American birds, 1.3 metres (4^1/$_4$ feet) long and with a wing-span of nearly 2.5 metres (over 8 feet).

POWER COMPANY PROTECTS CROCODILE

The American crocodile (*Crocodylus acutus*), too, is classified officially as 'endangered'. Crocodiles are animals mainly of the Old World, their New World counterparts being the alligators and caimans, but *C. acutus* is a true crocodile, now so diminished in numbers that it is almost certain to become extinct over most of its range, and would face total extinction were it not for the protection it is afforded in Florida. There may be no more than 200 to 400 American crocodiles in existence and, because they do not start breeding until they are about ten years old, this population may include as few as twenty-five breeding females. In 1977, crocodiles were discovered at Turkey Point, on land belonging to the Florida Power and Light Company, and nests and more than forty young were

... the American crocodile will survive beside the Florida power station ...

discovered later. The animals are studied closely and their movements monitored by radio tracking, and it has been found that they build their nests beside the artificial canals carrying cooling water in preference to more natural surroundings nearby. The canal banks have been modified slightly to provide attractive nesting positions at intervals along them, and it now seems at least possible that the American crocodile will survive beside the Florida power station even if it dies out everywhere else.

SPACE SHUTTLES AND MANATEES

Not far from the crocodiles' nesting sites another endangered species is being protected. The West Indian manatee (*Trichechus manatus*) occurs throughout the tropics along the eastern coasts of North, Central, and South America, but it has suffered greatly from loss of habitat, from hunting for its meat, and more recently from the usually fatal injuries sustained in accidents with the propellers of powerboats. At the Kennedy Space Center, NASA maintains freshwater sites

for them which they use and seem to enjoy although no one knows whether manatees need fresh water for their survival, and warm water discharged from the Frontenac power plant, near Cape Canaveral, provides them with wintering sites, for manatees cannot tolerate cold water. The Florida Power and Light Company also encourages manatees and maintains sites for them.

SAVING THE BIRDS

Tinamous are ground-nesting, dumpy little birds, rather like partridges — and often called partridges — but found only in Central and South America. They have been hunted extensively for their meat and their numbers greatly reduced. At Berazategui, in Buenos Aires Province, Argentina, EBAS (Estación Biológica de

Manatees (Trichechus manatus) *basking in the warm water discharged from the Florida Power and Light Company plant.*

Greater flamingoes

The flamingo is one of the most spectacular of all birds. Its fame rests on its large size, its colour which ranges from almost white through shades of pink to bright red, and on its gregariousness which leads it to nest and feed in large colonies. Flamingoes are related to storks and herons, aquatic birds with long necks and long legs with webbed feet, but their method of feeding is highly specialized and this may render them especially vulnerable to developments that deprive them of the only conditions in which they can survive. (The lesser flamingo, *Phoeniconaias minor,* feeds on cyanobacteria.)

Herons and storks feed on a wide variety of small animals — not all of them caught in water — which they hunt by walking forward slowly, then making a stabbing movement. They require clear water in which they can see prey. The flamingo works differently. It shuffles forward, stirring up the mud on the bottom of shallow water and disturbing small invertebrate animals. Its bill has an almost right-angle bend so that, when it is lowered into the water, the outermost section of the bill is horizontal. This outermost section contains a delicate arrangement of fine plates that form a filter. The flamingo fills its bill with muddy water and uses its large, powerful tongue as a piston to push the water past the filter, trapping and then swallowing any small animals that are present. It can feed in no other way so, while to some extent herons and storks can adapt to change, the flamingo is trapped. If it cannot find shallow water with a muddy bottom rich in invertebrates, it is doomed to starve.

A FLAMINGO SANCTUARY

Flamingoes occur in low latitudes throughout the world, and there are several species, but the most brightly coloured is the American race of the greater flamingo (*Phoenicopterus ruber ruber*). Although very rare in the United States, it feeds on mudflats along the Atlantic and Gulf coasts and around the islands of the Caribbean where, to the north-west of the coastal marshes near Caracas, Venezuela, lies the island of Bonaire, in the Netherlands Antilles. That is where the Antilles International Salt Company produces salt by solar evaporation in lagoons made for the purpose. In the 1960s, fears that salt production would harm the flamingoes led the company to collaborate with international conservation organizations in establishing a flamingo sanctuary on the industrial site. Flamingoes first bred there in 1969-70, and many young have been raised in the sanctuary in the years since.

Greater flamingoes (Phoenicopterus ruber) *swim and fly well. They are seen here in the Camargue, at the northern limit of their range, where they thrive among the brine lagoons.*

Flamingoes at dusk in the Camargue. They are highly social birds and a colony can number many thousands.

The flamingoes feed mainly on brine flies (*Ephydra cinerea*) and brine shrimps (*Artemia salina*) the populations of which have been somewhat reduced because of alterations in the salinity of the water caused by the industrial operation. To create its shallow lagoons, however, the company has flooded land with sea water and so increased greatly the total feeding area available to the birds. As more is learned about the precise physical, chemical, and biological requirements of this extraordinarily specialized bird, ways may be found to improve its habitat on Bonaire. Meanwhile it continues to breed successfully under conditions provided by this collaboration between an industrial company and conservationists.

A spiny-cheeked honeyeater in Australia. Because they feed on nectar, honeyeaters are thought to be important pollinators.

Aves Silvestres) has been established to study one particular species, the red tinamou, or partridge (*Rynchotus rufuscens*) which is of special interest partly because it is a popular game bird and partly, from an ethological point of view, because it is the male that hatches the eggs. The aim is to learn enough about the bird to allow a breeding programme to be instituted, and eventually to re-introduce it to the habitats, throughout Argentina, from which it has disappeared.

The Biological Station is a joint venture involving the Ministry of Agrarian Matters of the Buenos Aires Province, two organizations concerned with hunting and conservation, an association of businesses that supply sporting equipment, and ICI-Duperial which manufactures and markets sporting ammunition.

ICI promotes conservation in Argentina as elsewhere, and sponsors the Argentine

Wildlife Foundation, but it is not alone. Both the Wildlife Foundation and the Environment and Natural Resources Foundation have praised Cia. Petrolera Occidental de Argentina for the rigour of the studies it conducts of all the areas in

ICI promotes conservation in Argentina ...

which it plans to operate. Long before the machinery is moved in, the information the company has gathered allows it to prepare by planting trees, modifying the courses of streams and rivers and by taking whatever other steps are needed at least to protect and often to improve the local environment.

Thornbills are small, active, insectivorous birds, sometimes placed in the same family (Sylviidae) as European warblers but more usually in the Acanthizidae, the mainly Australian and New Guinea family that also includes the bristlebirds and scrub wrens. There are only eleven species of thornbills (*Acanthiza*), all of them confined to Australia. The birds are basically brown, but with coloured rumps that give them their common names although, as with many warblers, it is often difficult to distinguish one species from another. The samphire thornbill (*A. iredalei*) is one of the less common species, and clearly worth protecting. It occurs in one of the best bird sanctuaries in Southern Australia, at the Dry Creek Saltworks near Adelaide. The site includes 3970 hectares (9810 acres) of lagoons used to produce salt by solar evaporation. Very early in the programme of industrial development, the lagoons were declared a bird sanctuary. Hunting was forbidden

Australian pelicans (Pelecanus conspicillatus), *seen here at Port Alma, also thrive in the Point Wilson reserve, owned by ICI.*

Whales

At one time, whaling yielded such a range of products that it could be argued that no part of the animal was wasted and the industry was economically essential. Today, there are substitutes for all whale products.

Whales were killed to provide ambergris, used to fix perfumes. Baleen was the 'whalebone' in corsets, and was used to make the ribs for umbrellas, riding crops, and other products. The skin made good-quality leather for bicycle saddles, shoes, and handbags. The oil was used in oil cloth, linoleum, printing inks and paint, to make crayons and candles, as well as in such food products as margarine and cooking fat. Sperm oil provided lubricants and cutting oils and, together with spermaceti, was used in many toiletries and cosmetics. The tendons were used as strings in tennis rackets and for surgical stitching, the bone to make shoe horns and ornaments, and collagen extracted from bone went into edible jellies, confectionery, and photographic film; the meat became pet food, the blood was used in adhesives; pharmaceutical products were obtained from endocrine and pituitary glands, the liver was a commercial source of vitamin A; the teeth were carved into ornaments and rivalled ivory as a material for making piano keys; and whatever remained was made into fertilizer.

Baleen whales feed by taking in a mouthful of water then forcing it out through their baleen plates which trap food items. This is the baleen from a grey whale (Eschtrichtius gibbosus).

A plantation covering more than 2020 hectares (5000 acres) where jojoba (Simmondsia chinensis) is being grown for its oil, an alternative to sperm oil.

CHEMICAL INDUSTRY SAVING THE WHALE

By the 1970s, the oil and chemical industries were developing substitutes, partly because of growing opposition to whaling and partly because the precise composition, and therefore the quality, of a natural product is more difficult to control than that of one synthesized industrially. Esso, for example, developed a cutting oil that was better at preventing corrosion and emulsified better than the sulphurized sperm oil it replaced. The Calber Chemical Company, of Philadelphia, developed gear oils that were better than sperm oils, and several other companies produced specialist oils to improve on and replace oils from whales.

The cosmetic industry shifted away from whale products, substituting vegetable waxes and synthetic esters for sperm oils and ambergris. First castor oil and then mineral oils replaced sperm oil that was used in combing wool to make worsted fabrics. Sperm oil is an ester — an organic compound formed by the reaction of an acid with an alcohol with the elimination of water — that exists as a liquid wax. Used in lubricants that must withstand extreme pressures, it is one of the most difficult whale products to synthesize, and the United States Government classified it as a strategic material and accumulated stockpiles.

The alternative to it is obtained from the jojoba shrub (*Simmondsia chinensis*) which grows wild in the arid parts of Mexico and the south-western United States. The plant is believed to live for 100 to 200 years, can regenerate lost limbs, can withstand drought and tolerate salt, and its seeds contain about 50 per cent of liquid wax by weight, although at present the crop yield is low.

Industry has made a very real contribution to the conservation of whales by rendering whale products unnecessary. Whatever arguments may be advanced to sustain whaling, it is no longer possible to maintain that whales are a unique source of essential materials.

and, of course, public access was restricted, thus reducing disturbance. Today, waders overwinter there in tens of thousands, and there are vast numbers of banded stilts as well as silver gulls and fairy terns nesting on the dykes and causeways, and many more species. The samphire thornbills live among the vegetation bordering tracks and paths, together with blue-and-white wrens (*Malurus leucopterus*) and there are also mangroves that support crested pigeons (*Ocyphaps lophotes*) and singing honey-eaters (*Lichenostomus virescens*). There are more birds at Dry Creek now than there were before industry moved in and developed the area. Indeed, ICI has published a guide, called *Birds of a Salt Field*, to the birds of Dry Creek.

A RARE PARROT AT POINT WILSON

Perhaps the most important Australian example of co-operation between industry and conservation is to be found in the very south of Victoria, at Point Wilson, south-west of Melbourne. Some years ago, ICI acquired 766 hectares (1893 acres) of land at Point Wilson on which it planned to build a chloro-alkali and petrochemical complex. The plans were postponed for commercial reasons but, by then, the area had been recognized by ornithologists to be of international importance to bird life. It is a place of marshes, lakes, and lagoons where waders and wildfowl feed in their tens of thousands. On a visit in April, 1981, ICI Ecology Officer Ken Smith estimated there were up to 80 000 pink-eared duck (*Malacorhynchus membranaceus*) present on the marshes, as well as nearly 200 freckled duck (*Stictonetta naevasa*) — a rare species that is seldom seen in such a dense concentration. There are white ibis (*Threskiornis molucca*) and up to 50 000 straw-necked ibises (*T. spinicollis*) have been counted roosting. On the lakes and lagoons there are Australian pelicans (*Pelecanus conspicillatus*) and literally thousands of black swans (*Cygnus atratus*). At the time of his visit, Smith estimated there was a total of between 120 000 and 175 000 waders and wildfowl present on the marshes and the open water. On this basis alone, Point Wilson is clearly one of the most important bird sanctuaries in Australia, but it has an even more impressive claim to protection, for it provides a wintering site for one of the world's rarest birds, the orange-bellied parrot (*Neophema chrysogaster*).

THE ORANGE-BELLIED PARROT

Like so many species, orange-bellied parrots have suffered greatly because of the conversion of their habitat to human uses, and, like so many parrot species, they have been hunted for sale as pets. Caged parrots may survive, indeed may live for many years, but they rarely have an opportunity to breed and to raise young. In the whole world, there may be no more than 100 orange-bellied parrots left, making this one of the rarest of all birds. They spend the Australian winter in the extreme south of Victoria, Australia. When seventy-three of these rare birds were counted at Point Wilson, and were found to spend up to eight winter months there, the ornithological importance of this site for a proposed ICI chemical complex was obvious.

ICI SPONSORSHIP

The company responded by initiating a series of very detailed ecological studies of the Point Wilson area and contributed $A23 000 to the World Wildlife Fund (now the World Wide Fund for Nature) for surveys of the species in Tasmania by

The Great Barrier Reef, one of the richest ecosystems in the world, has been declared a biosphere reserve. Industry is helping to conserve it but a threat remains from offshore oil fields.

the Tasmanian National Parks and Wildlife Service. The Tasmanian ecologists looked for breeding areas and, in November 1979, they discovered nests — the first ever recorded for this species. The studies made it possible to identify the areas in which the parrots feed in winter as well as their diet. They were found to depend heavily on a particular species of glasswort (*Salicornia quinqueflora*). The grazing of sheep was stopped within the feeding area because the sheep were reducing the availability of this food plant by up to 80 per cent. One aim of the feeding studies is to allow ICI ecologists to ensure that the building and operation of the chemical plant have no adverse effect on the food plants. Large numbers of native trees were planted to screen the feeding area from the working area to reduce disturbance.

In November, 1980, the Murtcaim Wildlife Area was designated, partly on land donated by ICI, as a reserve that includes the principal feeding areas for both the parrots and the large number of waders that congregate on the marshes. ICI Australia has taken an active interest in the reserve since it was first proposed and participates in its management.

So far, no industrial activity has taken place at Point Wilson. After the land had been acquired, commercial considerations caused further plans to be postponed, leaving ICI in charge of an important nature reserve on an industrial site without any industry. The plans have not been abandoned, however, and one day the factories will be built. By that time, the company will have sufficient information to allow the wildlife to be accommodated. The industrial complex will be so designed as to cause the least possible disturbance, especially to the orange-bellied parrots, and great care will be taken to avoid damaging the marshlands and areas of open water. Overhead wires and flare stacks will be located where the risk to flying birds is minimal. The entire operation will be planned, from its very inception, with the needs of the local environment in mind.

INDUSTRY PROVIDES FUNDS FOR WILDLIFE

Shell has also helped Australian conservation by making a grant towards the $A10 000 cost of surveying the country's flora partly to identify and assess the status of endangered species. MIM Holdings, a mining company, has donated $A20 000 towards the cost of establishing nature reserves in Queensland, where the company is based, and Broken Hill Pty Ltd has donated more than $A46 000 to help protect the wildlife of Raine Island, one of the innumerable islands lying along the Great Barrier Reef, but said to be of particular biological importance. One of the richest ecosystems in the world, the Great Barrier Reef has been declared a 'biosphere reserve' but it is only fair to point out that, despite the protection afforded by its official status and the help given by the more enlightened industrial companies, there are fears that it may suffer severe damage from offshore oil exploration and exploitation.

AN ENDANGERED MAMMAL

Not all the news is good, after all, and not all industrialists have yet learned to moderate their activities to make them ecologically sensitive. In tropical Australia, for example, the woodchip industry has clear-felled large areas of rainforest, and conservationists fear it may destroy the only remaining habitat of Leadbeater's possum (*Gymnobelideus leadbeateri*). Already declared extinct once, and then rediscovered, this is one of the most seriously endangered mammal species in the world. Near Portland, Victoria, rare plants and mammals are threatened by an aluminium smelter. We cannot celebrate an outright victory for conservation, but a list of battles won and progress made.

CONCLUSION
SUSTAINABLE DEVELOPMENT

Our modern concern over the fate of the environment probably began in the early 1960s. Rachel Carson's *Silent Spring*, published in 1963, drew public attention to the dangers of the careless or over-zealous use of pesticides, and triggered the birth of the popular environmental movement. That book was followed by many more, and eventually to the dire warnings contained in *The Limits to Growth* and to what amounted to a manifesto for reform in *The Ecologist*'s 'Blueprint for Survival', both published in 1972 — the year of the United Nations Conference on the Human Environment.

As the debate developed, it became evident that the issues involved fell into three broad categories: the depletion of natural flora and fauna, mainly through loss of habitat; environmental pollution; and the depletion of essential but non-renewable resources. For a time, environmentalists could do little more than react to the developments they saw. Trapped in a state of perpetual opposition, their views appeared much more negative than in fact they were. Yet their outlook, if not all of their diagnoses and prescriptions, gained great influence.

GLOBAL 2000

The issues were global in extent, affecting industrialized countries mainly but also the less-industrialized countries, as well as the political and economic relationships between the two. Clearly, action, even the monitoring that was necessary to identify and to quantify the changes that might be taking place, required international collaboration and the support of governments and intergovernmental institutions. In 1977, President Carter commissioned a projection to the end of the century of what would happen to the size of the world population, natural resources, and the global environment. The resulting report, published in 1980 as *Global 2000*, repeated many of the earlier warnings, but elsewhere the emphasis had changed. Serious attempts were being made to describe a world in which reasonable human needs could be satisfied and the disgracefully wide gap reduced between the living standards of the very rich and the very poor, but without destroying the natural environment and without eroding the resource base on which economic development must depend. The idea was born of 'sustainable development'.

This concept was the principal theme running through the *World Conservation Strategy*, published in 1980 by the International Union for Conservation of Nature and Natural Resources (IUCN) with assistance from the United Nations Environment Programme (UNEP) and the then World Wildlife Fund, and in collaboration with the Food and Agriculture Organization of the United Nations (FAO) and the United Nations Educational, Scientific and Cultural Organization (UNESCO). Presented formally to all governments and widely publicized, the *Strategy* had three aims: to maintain essential ecological processes and life-support systems; to preserve genetic diversity; and to ensure the sustainable utilization of species and ecosystems.

The single word that set it apart from

earlier environmentalist writing was 'utilization'. The *Strategy* accepted that resources must be exploited if the human population is to be fed, clothed, housed, and provided with the educational, medical, and other services that are

---

... *resources must be exploited if the human population is to be fed, clothed, housed, ...*

---

essential to a decent, dignified life in the modern world. It was a concept that included people and it allowed a place for the industries whose task it is to supply human material needs. It invited industrialists and their governments to consider ways in which industries might operate successfully while minimizing their adverse effects on the environment and conserving natural resources. This was an invitation to which industrial planners could respond.

ASSURING THE FUTURE

The theme was repeated in 1987 in *Our Common Future*, the report of The World Commission on Environment and Development chaired by the Norwegian Prime Minister, Gro Harlem Brundtland. In its 'overview', the Report referred to 'the possibility for a new era of economic growth, one that must be based on policies that sustain and expand the environmental resource base'. The Report defined 'sustainable development' as development that 'meets the needs of the present without compromising the ability of future generations to meet their own needs' and, in 1989, the idea was taken a step further by Professor David Pearce, the Director of the London Environmental Economics Centre. He sought to formalize an old environmentalist concept, of 'environmental capital' in ways that might bring it within the scope of conventional economic studies and assessments. If that could be achieved, 'sustainable development' would occur if each generation passed on to the next a stock of assets no smaller than the stock it inherited, because the assets would include environmental as well as artificial capital.

THE PRICE OF CLEAN AIR

Translating the developmental and economic theory into practical policies is much more difficult than it may appear. It requires us to attach conventional and probably monetary values to 'goods' such as clean air and water, sunlight, a stable climate, and diverse natural communities, that are not bought and sold and so are, literally, 'priceless'. In some cases, at least, Pearce believes prices can be calculated. He has quoted the $7000 which is estimated to be the value of fruit and latex from 1 hectare (2.5 acres) of Peruvian rain forest, for example, compared with the $1000 value of the standing timber, to show that conserving the forest may be justifiable on purely economic grounds. He goes further, by suggesting we apply 'existence values'. These are the prices ordinary people are prepared to pay, in cash, for an assurance that a particular habitat or species will continue to exist.

... *minimizing their adverse effects ...*

Research has shown, for example, that some species, such as blue whales and sea otters, are 'worth' about $8 each and that air clear enough to see the Grand Canyon is worth $22 — and these values are per person for an entire country or, in the case of such animals as whales, for all the industrialized countries.

Industrialists, however, cannot delay their plans while details of the theory are resolved. They must make do with such information as they have and, where definitions and concepts are lacking, they may have to supply their own. Some of these are peculiar to industry but others are little different from those accepted by environmentalists and conservationists. The environment itself, for example, can be valued for the raw materials and resources it provides, but this essentially industrial view does not preclude the wise husbanding and conservation of those resources. It can be valued as a dynamic system that cycles nutrients and detoxifies harmful substances, and industrialists and environmentalists will agree that disruption of that system is harmful to both their interests. It can be valued for its amenity and aesthetic value, including its wildlife — a more obviously conservationist view but one of which modern industry must take account.

Industry must extract and process raw materials — for that is what industry does — and it must do so profitably. An unprofitable enterprise cannot survive, and an industrial operation that is abandoned before its completion is likely to cause much more environmental disruption than one that brings its plans — including environmental restoration — to fruition.

MULTI-NATIONAL CONCERNS

Many environmental concerns are global in extent and long-term in duration. Industry has been accused of seeking local, short-term benefits with too little regard for wider, long-term consequences but, as a generalization, this is unfair. Industry is international. The factory we see in our own neighbourhood, affecting the local environment, is quite likely to be related commercially to factories in other parts of the world, and there is usually a level in the managerial hierarchy at which the local environmental effects of all these operations combine to form a company environmental policy with global dimensions. A factory represents a large amount of invested capital and, if its products are capable of affecting the environment directly, large sums of money will have been spent to make sure they can cause no harm. The need to plan the return on this investment over the anticipated lifetime of the factory or product means industry has no choice but to take a long-term view.

A PROBLEM SHARED...

With a little rephrasing, these amount to areas of shared interest between industrialists and environmentalists that provide the basis for a common agenda, and that agenda will include sustainable development. There is also a shared interest in adopting a scientific approach to environmental matters. Both sides in the debate must be able to identify environmental costs and benefits precisely, to allocate priorities to perceived hazards, and to understand the technological and commercial constraints on what can be achieved. Industry now recognizes that perceptions change over the years as our knowledge of the environment and public expectations increase, and environmentalists are coming to realize that it may take time to achieve improvements everyone agrees are desirable.

At a practical level, the control of emissions into air and water began long ago, of course, and proceeds steadily as the technologies improve for measuring concentrations of pollutants and for disposing of them safely. In most cases emission limits are set by law, but a main purpose of the law is not so much to restrict industrial activities as to guarantee equity by requiring that all companies observe the standards attained by the most responsible. This avoids a situation in which an irresponsible manufacturer might reduce operating costs by failing to clean effluents and so gain an unfair competitive advantage. Good laws of any kind, after all, exist only to bring the behaviour of an antisocial minority into line with what the majority willingly accepts. Most of us do not refrain from killing or stealing merely because the law forbids it!

As the many examples described in this book have shown, there is nothing novel in the idea that factories should be designed and operated in such a way as to protect the wildlife in their vicinity. Some industrial sites include nature reserves, managed in collaboration with conservation organizations, where protection is afforded to rare or endangered species or to valuable habitats. Collaboration is sometimes expanded into a general statement of industry policy or a formal agreement. In Britain, for example, the Opencast Executive of British Coal and the Nature Conservancy Council signed a memorandum in July, 1989, committing them 'to retain and enhance areas of nature conservation importance and wildlife associated with them within the wider countryside of coalfields'.

During the 1960s and '70s, as British farming became more dependent on the use of agricultural chemicals and large machines, a conflict developed between farmers and conservationists. As in most intense disagreements, each side was largely ignorant of the legitimate concerns of the other. Farming and Wildlife Advisory Groups (FWAGs) were formed locally, eventually throughout the country, to provide forums in which farmers and conservationists could discuss the issues that divided them and attempt to reach compromises. The FWAGs were very successful. Conservationists learned more about the economic pressures to which farmers are subjected but, at the same time, they awakened an interest in wildlife among farmers, many of whom were helped to design areas of valuable

habitat on their land. Both sides accepted the need to compromise, and the standard of conservation on farms improved at little or no cost to the farmers.

Now that approach has been extended to other industries. In Cleveland, the Nature Conservancy Council, local authorities, and local industries have joined together to form the first Industry Nature Conservation Association (INCA). INCA consists of a small body of people with wide experience in industry and in nature conservation that aims to encourage companies to adopt the best conservation practices and to make environmental responsibility part of the policy of every company, so conservation is incorporated into internal training schemes together with safety, pollution abatement, and more general environmental protection. By providing a link between industry and commerce and skilled conservationists, INCA hopes to make each side more fully aware not only of the needs and limitations of the other, but also of the possibilities for reconciling those needs.

The formation of INCA was welcomed by the Royal Society for the Protection of Birds and by the Royal Society for Nature Conservation, as well as by the Confederation of British Industry, Fine Organics Limited, a large chemical company, Tioxide Group which manufactures titanium dioxide pigment, Ocean Environmental Management Limited, engaged in the transport and disposal of wastes, ICI, Phillips Petroleum, and BASF Chemicals. In time, its founders hope to expand the INCA collaboration to the whole of Britain and eventually, perhaps, into other EEC member countries.

A HEALTHIER WORLD

Like every other species, we humans modify our surroundings to make them more hospitable. Industry contributes to this modification but 'industry' is not something apart, distinct from society.

Industry comprises people, members of society no different from anyone else, and, like everyone else, they hope that the work they do enriches human life. They have achieved much. In the industrialized countries, most of us are better fed, better clothed, and better housed than our ancestors were or than many people are in the less-industrialized countries. We are healthier and fewer of us die in infancy or childhood. We must hope that these benefits will be extended to everyone in the world, and we are aware of the need of others mainly because we are better informed about the world than people have been at any time in the past. The wealth produced by industry allows us to make education available to everyone, and industry has provided the machinery — printing, radio, film, and television — by which information can be disseminated widely and rapidly.

It is that increasing awareness of the world in which we live, to which those who work in industry have contributed significantly, which now warns us of environmental dangers. Some of those dangers, although by no means all of them, arise from our industrial activities.

As the need for reform becomes apparent and the means for implementing it becomes available, the necessary changes are being made in factories.

The divergence of view between industrialists and environmentalists is more apparent than real for, if economic development cannot be sustained, everyone will suffer. Both groups share an interest in averting global environmental catastrophes, in reducing levels of pollution, and in conserving resources, natural habitats, and species. Remove their labels and 'industrialists' and 'environmentalists' are revealed as ordinary people, members of the same society, who share the opinions and values of that society. The resolution of their differences demands their collaboration. This has begun and it will develop and expand as the participants realize the true extent of their common agenda.

It will take time for the collaboration to bear fruit. When it does, we will have achieved a greater degree of harmony between two groups of interests in society and a new and sustainable level of harmony not only between industry and our planet, but also between human beings and the planet.

Index

Picture Credits